Shehzad Hussain

dian

recipe photography Graham Kirk

Shehzad Husain's

easy indian

cookery   hamlyn

HAM

notes

1 *All recipes serve 4, if served as part of an Indian meal comprising several dishes, unless otherwise stated.*
2 *Both metric and imperial measurements have been given in all recipes. Use one set of measurements only and not a mixture of both.*
3 *Standard level spoon measurements are used in all recipes.*
1 tablespoon = one 15 ml spoon
1 teaspoon = one 5 ml spoon
4 *Eggs should be medium unless otherwise stated.*
5 *Milk should be full fat unless otherwise stated.*
6 *Pepper should be freshly ground black pepper unless otherwise stated.*
7 *Fresh herbs should be used unless otherwise stated. If unavailable use dried herbs as an alternative but halve the quantities stated.*
8 *Ovens should be preheated to the specific temperature – if using a fan-assisted oven follow the manufacturer's instructions for adjusting the time and the temperature.*

author's acknowledgements

I wish to thank my husband Arif and my children Humaira, Sumra and Asim for their cooperation throughout, and my special thanks to Humaira for her help. I would also like to say thank you to my dear friend Mina for giving me her Gulgalay recipe.

acknowledgements

Publishing Director: Laura Bamford
Art Director: Keith Martin
Senior Designer: Louise Leffler
Designer: Les Needham
Commissioning Editor: Nicola Hill
Senior Editor: Sasha Judelson
Editor: Anne Crane
Editorial Assistant: Katey Day
Production Controller: Melanie Frantz
Indexer: Hilary Bird
Recipe Photography: Graham Kirk
Home Economist: Bridget Sargeson
Stylist: Helen Payne

First published in Great Britain in 1997 by Hamlyn
an imprint of Octopus Publishing Group Ltd.
2–4 Heron Quays, London E14 4JP

Text copyright © 1997 Shehzad Husain
Photography and Design copyright © 1997 Octopus Publishing Group Ltd.

This paperback edition first published in 1999.

ISBN 0 600 59862 4

A CIP catalogue record for this book is available from the British Library
Produced by Toppan, Hong Kong
Printed in China

contents

introduction

For those of Indian and Pakistani origin, the art of cooking is usually passed on from generation to generation. Although traditional methods and combinations of flavours have been used for centuries, there is always something new to try.

There have been many influences on the eating habits and the prefered flavours of the various groups throughout the whole of the sub-continent; the food eaten in the north, for example, differs quite considerably from that of the south. The people of the north, which is a wheat-growing area, prefer breads such as chapati, paratas or naan as their staple diet, while rice, which is grown in many of the southern states, is preferred by southerners. Muslims are the meat-eating people of India but, for religious reasons, they do not eat anything derived from the pig, which is considered unclean. Hindus, a vast number of whom are vegetarians, are forbidden to eat beef because they regard the cow as sacred.

Spices and herbs have been used to flavour food for thousands of years in the east, and India has been an important source of spices for western nations for centuries, yet it is only in the last twenty years or so that the majority of people in the west have become generally aware of our spicy cuisine. This may well be because people travel so extensively nowadays that the world has become a smaller place and people have been able to taste a variety of unfamiliar dishes. The Indian and Pakistani communities who have settled in Britain have preserved their own culture and eating habits but through the trading systems they have set up for specialist ingredients and utensils, they have made real Indian cookery possible on a very wide

scale. There has also been a rapid proliferation of Indian and Pakistani restaurants in towns and cities throughout the world and the steady growth of sections in supermarkets selling good quality chilled and frozen Indian and Pakistani meals.

I have tried to make the recipes in this book as easy to follow as possible. Whether or not you have cooked Indian food before, you will find that most of the recipes are straightforward and do not require any specialist skills or experience. There is little very last minute preparation, which makes cooking much simpler, especially if you are entertaining. The majority of dishes can be made in advance and will keep for 2–3 days in the refrigerator, while the vegetarian dishes will keep for a little longer. It is also a good idea to freeze popular standby items such as kebabs.

Although there are no hard and fast rules about how Indian meals should be served, restaurants have become accustomed to people eating a starter, so I have suggested a number of dishes which could be served as a first course if you are entertaining.

A typical daily meal in a non-vegetarian Indian household consists of one lamb or chicken curry, one vegetable curry or a dhaal (lentil) dish, plus a salad, a raita or a kachumer and rice, and either chapatis or paratas.

You may find adding a little variety makes a vegetarian meal more interesting. There could be Haandi Cauliflower Bhujia with Fried Potatoes (see page 82) or some type of pulse or lentil dish for protein and maybe chapatis or puris. Most Indian households will also have a wide selection of pickles and chutneys to perk up any kind of meal. Poppadums are not necessarily eaten everyday, but they are often served as an accompaniment, or as a starter with pickles and chutneys, as served in many Indian restaurants.

spices As far as the heat levels of curry go, it really depends how hot you like your food. If you are keen on very hot dishes, then I suggest you simply increase the amount of chilli powder. On the other hand, if you prefer milder curries, then remove the seeds of the green and red chillies. I would not suggest you omit them entirely as they add a nice aroma. Take care when you handle fresh or dried chillies, either wear rubber gloves or wash your hands, knives and chopping boards thoroughly when you have finished, as they contain volatile oils which can burn, particularly if they come into contact with sensitive areas, especially around the eyes.

As far as stocking up on spices goes, you do not have to spend very much unless you are cooking Indian and Pakistani food on a daily basis, in which case you should probably buy slightly larger quantities. However, since most good high street supermarkets now stock the vast majority of the spices and fresh items you will need, you really can shop as and when you require the ingredients. Do not try to keep too many spices as they soon lose their aroma and flavour.

There are a number of ways you can use spices – whole or ground, roasted or fried, or mixed. Each spice can alter the flavour of a dish and different combinations of several spices can produce a variety of colours and textures. The quantities of spices given in the recipes in this book are merely a guide, so feel free to increase or decrease the quantities if you wish.

making a tarka or baghaar A tarka or baghaar is, I believe, used only in Indian and Pakistani cooking. Oil or ghee is heated to a very high temperature without burning, and spices, onions and herbs are dropped into the oil, immediately changing colour and becoming highly aromatic. The seasoned oil is then removed from the heat and poured over the dish, rather like a dressing. Sometimes uncooked food is added to the heated oil too, and sautéed or simmered. You will find full instructions for making a tarka with the relevant recipes.

ginger and garlic Because ginger and garlic are used in a lot of curries, and as it takes time and effort to peel and chop them, I suggest you take about 250 g (8 oz) of each one and soak them separately in water overnight to make them easier to peel. The following day, peel and grind them separately in a food processor, adding a little more water to make a pulp. The pulps can be stored separately in airtight containers in a cool place for up to a month, to be used when you need them.

papaya This is the best meat tenderizer I know. To make papaya pulp, peel and discard the seeds from a papaya (an unripe one is preferable otherwise it will add a sweet flavour to your curry) then roughly chop the flesh and place it in a food processor, adding about 2 tablespoons of water to make a paste. Unused papaya pulp can be frozen for use another time.

freezing Indian food Before I go on holiday I usually cook and freeze a few curries for my return. Since it is not always easy to buy fresh coriander, this can can be bought in large quantities when it is in season and chopped and frozen in small batches for later use.

a good curry In the majority of cases the secret of a good curry depends on how well you brown the onions at the beginning. This requires patience, especially if you are cooking a large quantity. Heat the oil first, add the onions, then lower the heat so the onions become a nice golden brown without burning. Do not stir them too much as this draws moisture from them and makes them more difficult to fry, just stir very occasionally with a wooden spoon.

Once the onions are browned, add the spices, meat or other ingredients and mix and coat by the bhoonoing method (stirring and frying in semicircular movements, scraping the bottom of the pan) – this is essential for a good result. Finally, always taste the food and adjust the seasoning according to your own taste. You should use the recipes as guidelines and not as prescriptions. Only you know how you want the food to taste, so don't be afraid to add your own touch.

It is always a good idea, particularly if you are not familiar with Indian cooking, to set out all the spices you need before you start cooking and keep them in handy small bowls.

thickening sauces We seldom use any thickening agents in our curries and rely solely on onions and spices to make a thick sauce. Yogurt is also used to thicken some curries and give a thick creamy texture. Cream is added to some Indian dishes nowadays and so is Greek yogurt.

cooking equipment

Most of the kitchen equipment you need for cooking Indian food is more than likely already in your kitchen. Good quality, heavy-based saucepans, a frying pan, a slotted spoon, spatulas and wooden spoons are all essentials, as are sharp knives, measuring spoons and jugs, a garlic press, a rolling pin and an accurate set of kitchen scales. A food processor and liquidizer are as important to the Indian cook as they are to their western equivalent.

haandi These curiously shaped traditional cooking pots have always been popular in India and Pakistan, and are now available in the west. They come in all sizes, and are made from copper, clay and, more recently, stainless steel.

karahi Sometimes spelt kadhai or karihai, this is a deep frying pan with handles on both sides, rather like a straight-sided wok. It is most commonly made of iron, aluminium or stainless steel. A Chinese wok or a large, good quality frying pan can be used as a substitute.

balti pans Now that balti cooking is becoming so popular in the west, balti pans are widely available. They are almost the same as the karahi, which can be used as a substitute. Balti pans are very similar in shape to a wok.

thawa A slightly concave frying pan or griddle, usually made of cast iron, this is used for cooking paratas and chapatis and for roasting spices. An ordinary frying pan can be used as a substitute. A small one, 12 cm (5 inches) in diameter, is best for roasting spices.

spice box As an Indian cook uses spices every day, they are stored in a spice box by the stove and used before they have time to go stale. Many spice boxes are very attractive, but do be sure they are airtight as well. I suggest you always keep your spices in airtight containers and try to replace them from time to time. I have suggested ground spices in most recipes in this book and these are available from most supermarkets. However, if you want to use really fresh ground spices to achieve a fresher taste, I suggest you buy whole spices in small quantities and grind them in a spice grinder before use.

spice grinder In the past, the traditional Indian cook would grind spices on a grinding stone. Simple alternatives to this are a pestle and mortar or even a rolling pin, but the best modern substitute is an electric spice grinder, which is ideal for the small quantities often used in home curries, or even a coffee grinder, used only for grinding spices, thus avoiding any spicy flavoured coffee.

mango powder

chilli powder

coriander seeds

tamarind

black cardamom

white sesame seeds

dried chillies

allspice

crushed red chillies

fenugreek

poppy seed

curry leaves

fennel seeds

cumin seeds

turmeric

coconut powder

black cumin seeds

ground turmeric

green cardamom

black onion seeds

saffron strands

garam masala

cinnamon sticks

ground ginger

an abc of ingredients

asafoetida A pale yellow spice with a strong, distinctive flavour, used in small quantities to enhance other flavours in a dish.

aamchoor Sour-tasting mango powder made from dried raw mangoes. It is sold in jars.

ata *see* Wholemeal flour.

besun *see* Gram flour.

bhoonay chanay Dried roasted chick peas.

bitter gourd *(karela)* A bitter tasting gourd with a very knobbly skin. It should be peeled and salted or blanched before cooking to reduce the bitter flavour.

bundi Small, round, pearl-sized drops made from green lentil flour, usually soaked in water before use.

cardamom *(elaichi)* This spice, native to India, is considered the second most expensive (after saffron). The pods can be used with or without their husks and have a slightly pungent but very aromatic taste. They come in three varieties: green, white and black. The green and white pods can be used in both sweet and savoury dishes or to flavour rice; the black pods, which are larger are used only in savoury dishes.

cassia *see* Cinnamon.

cayenne pepper *see* Chilli powder.

chana dhaal Similar in appearance to moong dhaal (yellow split peas) – this lentil has slightly less shiny grains. It is used as a binding agent and makes an attractive dish as it does not lose its colour when cooked.

chana dhaal flour *see* Gram flour.

chapati flour *see* Wholemeal flour.

chilli powder *(laal mirch)* or cayenne pepper.

powdered dried red chillies A very fiery spice, to be used with caution.

chillies, dried red *(sabath sookhi laal mirch)* These pods, available whole or crushed, are extremely fiery and should be used with caution; their effect can be toned down slightly by removing the seeds. Dried chillies are usually fried in oil before use.

chillies, fresh green *(hari mirch)* Highly aromatic in flavour, these are used both in cooking and as a garnish. Though now so closely identified with Indian cooking, they were not introduced to the country until the 16th century, by the Portuguese. The seeds, which are the hottest part, may be removed if desired, by slitting the chilli down the middle. Never touch your face, especially your eyes or nose, during or after handling chillies; even after washing your hands as it will sting.

cinnamon *(dhalchini)* One of the earliest-known spices, cinnamon comes from the bark of a tree grown mainly in Sri Lanka. It has an aromatic and sweet flavour. Sold both in powdered form and as sticks. The bark of the tree from which cinnamon comes is sold as cassia bark.

cloves *(laung)* Used to flavour many sweet and savoury dishes; usually added whole. A whole clove is sometimes used to seal a betel leaf for serving after an Indian meal *(see* Paan).

coconut *(khopra or narial)* Used to flavour sweet or savoury dishes, fresh coconuts can often be bought in supermarkets. Desiccated coconut and creamed coconut are also available and for most dishes make acceptable substitutes. Coconut is sometimes toasted before cooking.

coriander, fresh *(hara dhania)* A fragrant herb used as an ingredient and as a garnish. The lacy, green leaves are also known as cilantro and Chinese parsley.

coriander seeds *(dhania)* This aromatic spice has a pungent, slightly lemony flavour. The seeds are used widely, either coarsely ground or powdered, in meat, fish and poultry dishes.

corn oil Less fattening than other oils, especially ghee, and also odourless, this is my preferred cooking oil.

cumin, ground *(safaid zeera)* A rather musty-smelling spice in its raw state, widely used for flavouring lentils and vegetable curries. Its flavour comes into its own when roasted or fried.

cumin seeds *(shah zeera)* Black cumin seeds, which have a strong aromatic flavour, are used to flavour curries and rice. White cumin seeds cannot be used as a substitute for black cumin seeds.

curry leaves *(kari patta)* Similar in appearance to bay leaves but very different in flavour. Available fresh (occasionally) or dried, curry leaves are used to flavour lentil dishes and vegetable curries.

doodi *(kaddu)* A vegetable – a member of the squash family. It is shaped rather like a curved courgette and is generally pale green in colour. Marrow, squash or courgettes can be substituted, if unavailable.

fennel seeds *(sonfe)* Similar to white cumin, these have a sweet anise taste and are used to flavour certain curries. They can also be chewed (as betel nut and cardamom are) after a spicy meal as a mouth freshener.

fenugreek *(methi)* The flavour of the whole, dried, flat yellow seeds, a little bitter in taste, improves when they are lightly fried. The seeds are very hard and can only be ground with a pestle and mortar or electric spice grinder. They are an essential ingredient in curry powders and pastes. Fresh fenugreek, sold in bunches, has very small leaves and is used to flavour both meat and vegetarian dishes.

garam masala A mixture of spices which can either be made up at home from freshly ground spices or bought ready made. There is no set formula, but a typical mixture might include black cumin seeds, peppercorns, cloves, cinnamon and black cardamom. To make your own mixture, grind together a 2.5 cm (1 inch) piece of cinnamon stick, 3 cloves, 3 black peppercorns, 2 black cardamoms (with husks removed) and 2 teaspoons black cumin seeds. If desired, multiply the quantities, grind and store in an airtight jar for future use.

garlic *(lassun)* This very useful flavouring is frequently used in curries, especially with ginger. It can be puréed in large quantities in a food processor and kept in an airtight container in the refrigerator. Whole garlic cloves are sometimes added to lentil dishes.

ghee (clarified butter) There are two kinds: pure (a dairy product) and vegetable. Though it was once a matter of pride to claim that everything served in one's household was cooked in pure ghee, it is in fact quite high in cholesterol, so from the health standpoint it may be better to use vegetable ghee or vegetable oil wherever possible (the majority of curries are cooked in oil). To make pure ghee at home, melt 250 g (8 oz) butter in a heavy saucepan and allow to simmer for 10–12 minutes. Once the milky white froth has turned golden, strain (preferably through muslin) and store in a jar.

gram flour (besun or chana dhaal flour) Made from lentils, gram flour is used to make pakoras, and can also be used as a binding agent. This kind of flour is also useful for people who are allergic to gluten, a component of all wheat products.

kaddu see Doodi.

karela see Bitter gourd.

kewra water This is the essence of pandanus or screwpine, used to flavour sweet dishes and sometimes rice. It is sold in small bottles. Its scent is reminiscent of vanilla essence, a little of which may be substituted.

mace see Nutmeg.

mango powder see Aamchoor.

masoor dhaal Small, round and pale orange in colour, these split lentils are stocked by all supermarkets, labelled simply 'lentils' or 'red lentils'.

mooli From the same family as the radish; long, rather like a cucumber, and white, mooli has a lovely flavour and a crunchy texture. It goes well with carrot.

moong dhaal A tear-drop-shaped yellow split lentil, more popular in northern India than in the south.

mustard oil Often used in Bengali dishes, especially for cooking fish.

mustard seeds (sarson ke beenji rai) These small round seeds, either black, brown, yellow or white, are rather sharp in flavour. Black mustard seeds are the most pungent variety and white mustard seeds the least. Black mustard seeds are used in curries, chutneys and pickles.

nutmeg (jaifal) Nutmeg, a native of Indonesia, is sweet and aromatic. It is most pungent when freshly grated. Mace, with its slightly more subtle flavour, is the lacy covering on the nutmeg kernel.

okra A small, green, sweet variety of banana, pointed at one end and containing numerous small white seeds. Often used as a thickener.

onion seeds (kalongi) Black in colour and triangular in shape, these little seeds are used for both pickles and vegetable curries.

paan Betel leaf wrapped around calcium paste, cardamom and fennel seeds, etc., and held together with a clove and sometimes covered with varq. Served at the end of the meal as a mouth-freshener. It may contain tobacco, in which case it can be addictive. It can be bought or made at home.

paprika This powder, made from dried sweet red pepper, is known as a hot spice, though it is much less fiery than chilli pepper. Paprika is not used much in Indian cookery.

pepper Whenever possible, use freshly ground black pepper in all Indian cookery.

pistachio nuts Widely used in Indian desserts, these are not the salty type sold in their shells but the shelled ones sold in packets at all Indian and Pakistani grocers. They have a mild, slightly sweet taste.

poppy seeds (khush khush) These dried whole seeds are always better when toasted. They are used, often whole, to flavour curries. Although they are from the opium poppy, they do not contain opium.

root ginger (adrak, fresh ginger, green ginger) One of the most popular flavourings in India and also one of the oldest, ginger is an important ingredient in many curries. It should always be peeled before use and can be puréed in a food processor. It is used in both savoury and sweet dishes. Dried powdered ginger (sontt) is also useful.

rose-water A liquid distilled from fragrant rose petals. This is used mainly to flavour sweetmeats.

saffron (zafran) The world's most expensive spice has a uniquely beautiful flavour and fragrance. Made from the stigmas of the saffron crocus, native to Asia Minor, each 500 g (1 lb) of saffron needs 60,000 stigmas. Fortunately, only a small quantity is needed to flavour or colour a dish, whether sweet or savoury. Saffron is sold as strands or in powder form.

sesame seeds (thill) Whole, flat, cream-coloured seeds, these are used to flavour curries. They are also known as benne seeds. When ground, sesame seeds can also be made into chutney.

set A spice mixture.

sev Very fine gram flour strands, used in bhel poori, which can be bought in Indian and Pakistani grocers.

sontt see Root ginger.

tamarind (imli) The dried pods of the tamarind, or Indian date. They are sour tasting and very sticky. Tamarind has to be soaked in hot water to extract the flavour. Though it is much stronger than lemon, lemon is often used as a substitute. Nowadays tamarind can be bought in paste form in jars: mix with a little water to bring it to a runny consistency.

toor dhaal Split pigeon peas; larger and more yellow than moong dhaal.

turmeric (haled) This yellow, bitter-tasting spice is sold ground. It is used mainly for colour, rather than flavour.

urid dhaal Though very similar in size and shape to moong dhaal, this lentil is white and a little drier when cooked. It is popular in northern India.

urid dhaal flour This very fine white flour is used for vadde (deep-fried dumplings), and for dosas (Indian rice pancakes).

varq Edible silver leaf used for decoration purposes. It is very delicate and should be handled carefully. Varq can be bought in sheets from Indian or Pakistani grocers, though you may have to order it.

wholemeal flour (ata) Chapati flour, available at any Indian or Pakistani grocers, is used to make chapatis, paratas and puris. Ordinary wholemeal flour, very well sieved, may also be used for Indian breads.

clockwise from bottom left: a spice box, a balti pan, a pestle and mortar and two haandi pots

chicken dishes

haandi chicken
with pineapple chunks

1 Reserve 6 of the cashew nuts and grind the rest in a spice grinder. Transfer to a mixing bowl. Dry roast the reserved cashews in a warmed frying pan for about 1½ minutes, moving the cashews around the pan while roasting.

2 Drain the juice from the pineapple and then stir the pineapple juice into the ground cashews.

3 Reserve the pineapple chunks for the garnish. Add the chicken pieces, ground coriander, chilli powder, garam masala, ginger, garlic, salt, ground cardamom, coconut milk and yogurt and stir to mix.

4 Heat the oil in a haandi or a heavy-based saucepan and fry the onions until golden brown.

5 Throw in the curry leaves, then add the chicken mixture and stir-fry for 5–7 minutes. Lower the heat, cover, and cook for 10 minutes.

6 Remove the lid, add the finely chopped fresh coriander and red chillies and stir-fry for 2 minutes. Serve garnished with the roasted cashew nuts and chunks of pineapple.

ingredients

50 g (2 oz) cashew nuts
1 x 227g (8 oz) can pineapple chunks in natural juice
500 g (1 lb) boneless, skinless chicken, cut into 2.5–3.5 cm (1–1½ inch) cubes
1 teaspoon ground coriander
1 teaspoon chilli powder
1 teaspoon garam masala
1 teaspoon ginger pulp
1 teaspoon garlic pulp
1 teaspoon salt
¼ teaspoon ground cardamom
175 ml (6 fl oz) coconut milk
2 tablespoons natural yogurt
4 tablespoons corn oil
2 onions, finely chopped
6 curry leaves
2 tablespoons finely chopped fresh coriander
2 fresh red chillies, finely diced

ingredients

1 tablespoon tomato purée
1 teaspoon ginger pulp
1 teaspoon garlic pulp
1½ teaspoons chilli powder
2 teaspoons mango powder
2 teaspoons ground coriander
1 teaspoon salt
1 teaspoon ground cumin
250–300 g (8–10 oz) boneless, skinless chicken breast, cut into small cubes
2 tablespoons cornflour
approximately 300 ml (½ pint) corn oil, for deep-frying

fried vegetables:
4 tablespoons corn oil
¼ teaspoon onion seeds
10 curry leaves
½ teaspoon coriander seeds, crushed, in a pestle and mortar
½ teaspoon cumin seeds
6 black peppercorns, crushed
1 teaspoon crushed dried red chillies,
8–10 baby courgettes
12–14 baby onions
125 g (4 oz) frozen green beans, defrosted
1 tablespoon chopped fresh coriander
12–14 cherry tomatoes

to garnish:
lemon wedges
fresh coriander (optional)

In this recipe, chicken pieces are lightly coated with spices and cornflour, then deep-fried and served with whole vegetables which have been fried separately with whole spices. A dry dish, it should be served with a wet dish, such as Haandi Lentils with Lemon Juice and Fresh Tomatoes (see page 87).

fried chicken
with whole baby vegetables
(Thali Huwi Murghi Aur Sabuth Sabzee)

1 In a small bowl, mix together the tomato purée, ginger, garlic, chilli powder, mango powder, ground coriander, salt and cumin.

2 With your hands, rub the spice mixture on to the chicken pieces. Sprinkle with the cornflour and toss to coat thoroughly.

3 Heat the corn oil for deep-frying in a karahi or deep frying pan and fry the chicken pieces, a few at a time, for 7–10 minutes. Remove from the pan with a slotted spoon and drain on kitchen paper. Set aside.

4 To cook the vegetables, heat 4 tablespoons of oil in a deep frying pan and fry the onion seeds, curry leaves, crushed coriander seeds, cumin seeds, black peppercorns and red chillies for about 1 minute, then add the baby courgettes, baby onions and green beans and stir-fry for 1½–2 minutes until the baby onions have browned slightly.

5 Add the cooked chicken pieces, fresh coriander and cherry tomatoes and cook for 2 minutes until heated through. Serve garnished with lemon wedges and more fresh coriander, if wished.

previous page from left to right: fried chicken with whole baby vegetables and haandi chicken with pineapple chunks

ingredients

500 g (1 lb) boneless, skinless chicken, cut into small pieces
3 tablespoons natural yogurt
1 teaspoon garam masala
1 teaspoon chilli powder
1 teaspoon ginger pulp
1 teaspoon garlic pulp
1 teaspoon salt
2 tablespoons lemon juice

sauce:
75 g (3 oz) unsalted butter
1 tablespoon corn oil
2 onions, diced
2 small fresh bay leaves
½ teaspoon ground cardamom
2 green cardamoms
1 teaspoon garam masala
1 teaspoon ginger pulp
1 teaspoon garlic pulp
1 teaspoon salt
1 teaspoon chilli powder
1 teaspoon natural yogurt
4 tablespoons single cream
4 tablespoons coconut milk
2 tablespoons ground almonds
1 teaspoon saffron strands, crushed
50 g (2 oz) sultanas

to garnish:
50 g (2 oz) flaked almonds
1 tablespoon finely chopped fresh coriander

The chicken pieces in this dish are grilled before being added to the rich sauce to give them a charcoal flavour. The sauce is fairly mild and the sultanas give it a sweet taste.

mughlai haandi chicken in a rich sauce

1 Put the chicken pieces into a large bowl. In a small bowl, mix together the yogurt, garam masala, chilli powder, ginger, garlic, salt and lemon juice. Pour the yogurt mixture over the chicken pieces and blend thoroughly. Cover and set aside in a cool place to marinate for at least 3 hours.

2 Remove the chicken pieces from the marinade. Place under a preheated hot grill. Cook the chicken pieces for about 10–15 minutes, turning and basting them once.

3 To make the sauce, melt the unsalted butter with the corn oil in a saucepan over a medium heat and fry the onions until golden brown. Using a slotted spoon, remove the diced onions from the pan, leaving as much fat as possible in the saucepan.

4 When cool, place the onions in a food processor and mince.

5 Return the onions to the saucepan and reheat. Add the bay leaves, ground and whole cardamom, garam masala, ginger pulp, garlic pulp, salt and chilli powder and stir-fry over a low heat for 1 minute. Remove the saucepan from the heat.

6 In a small bowl, mix together the yogurt, single cream, coconut milk, ground almonds and crushed saffron strands. Return the saucepan containing the onion mixture to the heat and then gradually add the creamy yogurt mixture, stirring with a wooden spoon. Bring the mixture slowly to the boil, then add half of the sultanas to the pan.

7 Transfer the sauce to a serving bowl. Drop the pieces into the sauce. Garnish with the remaining sultanas, the flaked almonds and finely chopped fresh coriander.

ingredients
3 tablespoons natural yogurt
1 teaspoon garam masala
1½ teaspoons ground coriander
1½ teaspoons chilli powder
1 tablespoon chopped fresh coriander
1 teaspoon garlic pulp
1 tablespoon corn oil
1½ teaspoons salt
500 g (1 lb) boneless, skinless chicken, cut into 5 cm (2 inch) pieces

sauce:
50 g (2 oz) unsalted butter
3 tablespoons corn oil
½ teaspoon mustard seeds
2 onions, finely diced
1 teaspoon garlic pulp
1 teaspoon ginger pulp
2 teaspoons ground coriander
1 teaspoon chilli powder
175 g (6 oz) button mushrooms
3 tablespoons lemon juice
1 teaspoon salt
8 tablespoons finely chopped fresh coriander
2 tablespoons Greek yogurt
175 ml (6 fl oz) single cream
2 fresh red chillies, diced, to garnish

This curry makes a delicious centrepiece at any dinner party. Although I have used boneless chicken pieces, you may also use pieces on the bone if you like.

balti chicken in a creamy lemon sauce

1 In a bowl, mix together the yogurt, garam masala, ground coriander, chilli powder, fresh coriander, garlic, corn oil and salt.
2 Pour the spice mixture over the chicken pieces, cover and leave to marinate for about 2 hours.
3 Meanwhile, make the sauce. In a balti pan, karahi or large saucepan, heat the butter with the corn oil and fry the mustard seeds for about 30 seconds. Add the onions and fry for 1½–2 minutes. Lower the heat and add the garlic, ginger, ground coriander, chilli powder, mushrooms, lemon juice, salt and half of the fresh coriander and stir-fry for at least 2 minutes. Stir in the Greek yogurt and cream and cook for a further 2–3 minutes. Set aside.
4 Place the marinated chicken pieces on a heatproof dish and set under a preheated medium grill. Grill for about 7 minutes, basting occasionally and turning at least twice.
5 Drop the chicken pieces into the sauce and cook over a medium heat for about 2 minutes.
6 Transfer to a warmed serving dish and serve, garnished with the remaining fresh coriander and the diced red chillies.

ingredients
5 tablespoons corn oil
2 onions, very finely diced
6–8 curry leaves
1 teaspoon ginger pulp
1 teaspoon garlic pulp
½ teaspoon turmeric
1 teaspoon chilli powder
½ teaspoon ground nutmeg
1 cinnamon stick
2 tablespoons lemon juice
250 ml (8 fl oz) coconut milk
1 x 1.25 kg (2½ lb) chicken, cut into 8–10 pieces
2 tablespoons chopped fresh coriander

spice paste:
1 teaspoon fennel seeds
2 teaspoons coriander seeds
1 teaspoon cumin seeds
4 green cardamoms
2 whole cloves
3 black peppercorns
1 tablespoon white poppy seeds
2 tablespoons desiccated coconut
3 tablespoons water

Traditionally all the whole spices in this recipe are dry-roasted. However, if you wish to take a short cut, use ready ground spices. Whichever method you choose, this is a very tasty and aromatic chicken curry, so do try it.

chicken in a coconut and fennel sauce

1 First make the spice paste. Heat a non-stick frying pan and dry-roast the whole spices and the coconut for a few seconds. Remove the pan from the heat and leave to cool for about 10 minutes, then grind the spices in a spice grinder. Turn into a bowl, pour in the water and work to a paste, set aside.
2 Heat the oil in a large saucepan, add the onions and curry leaves and fry until soft and golden brown.
3 While the onions are cooking, mix together the ginger, garlic, turmeric, chilli powder, nutmeg, cinnamon, lemon juice and coconut milk. Pour the mixture into the onions and stir-fry for about 2 minutes over a low heat.
4 Add the chicken pieces and coat well with the spicy sauce. Pour in the spice paste and stir thoroughly. If the mixture looks a bit dry, add about 150 ml (¼ pint) water, cover with a lid and cook for about 12–15 minutes.
5 Check to see that the chicken pieces are cooked through, then stir gently for 2 minutes. Stir in the fresh coriander and serve with rice or pasta.

opposite: balti chicken in a creamy lemon sauce

ingredients

1 x 1.25 kg (2½ lb) chicken,
   cut into 8–10 pieces
4 tablespoons Greek yogurt
1 tablespoon tomato purée
2 tablespoons ground almonds
1 tablespoon ground coconut
2 teaspoons ground coriander
1 teaspoon garam masala
1 teaspoon ginger pulp
1 teaspoon garlic pulp
1 teaspoon chilli powder
1 teaspoon salt
2 tablespoons lemon juice
4–5 tablespoons corn oil
4 green cardamoms
1 cinnamon stick
4–6 black peppercorns
¼ teaspoon black cumin
   seeds
2 onions, finely diced
150 ml (¼ pint) water
75 ml (3 fl oz) single cream
2 tablespoons chopped fresh
   coriander
2 fresh green chillies, chopped
   (optional)
2 tomatoes, skinned, deseeded
   and diced

Pasanda is traditionally made with lamb or beef. However, as chicken is very popular I have made it with chicken very successfully and I am sure you will enjoy it too. Although I have used a whole chicken, you may use boneless chicken pieces, if you wish.

creamy **chicken pasanda**

1 Place the chicken pieces in a large bowl. In a separate bowl beat together the Greek yogurt, tomato purée, ground almonds, ground coconut, ground coriander, garam masala, ginger, garlic, chilli powder, salt and lemon juice.
2 Blend the spice mixture into the chicken pieces, cover and leave to marinate for about 2 hours.
3 Heat the corn oil in a large saucepan, add the cardamoms, cinnamon stick, peppercorns and black cumin seeds and fry for about 30 seconds. Add the onions and fry until golden brown.
4 Add the chicken pieces and stir-fry for 3–5 minutes over a high heat. Lower the heat, stir in the water and cook, covered, for about 15 minutes, stirring at least once.
5 When the chicken is cooked, stir the mixture a few times, then stir in the cream and half of the fresh coriander and green chillies, if using. Transfer to a serving dish, and garnish with the remaining fresh coriander, green chillies and the diced tomato.

This recipe has been a great favourite on Indian restaurant menus for a long time. As with all traditional recipes, there are several versions; however, this is one of my favourite ones and very easy to follow. Ideal for a dinner party, serve it with any of the pulao rices or paratas in this book.

butter chicken

(Murgh Makhani)

1 Place the chicken pieces in a bowl.
2 Melt the butter with the oil in a haandi or heavy-based saucepan and fry the onions and bay leaf over a medium heat for about 2 minutes.
3 While the onions are cooking, beat the yogurt lightly and add the ginger, garlic, turmeric, chilli powder, ground cardamom, garam masala, salt and ground almonds. Pour the spice mixture on to the chicken and mix together.
4 Add the chicken mixture to the onions and stir to mix. Lower the heat, cover with a lid and cook for 12–15 minutes, stirring at least once.
5 Remove the lid and stir carefully. Add the diced red pepper, cream and fresh coriander. Serve directly from the haandi, if you like.

ingredients

1 x 1.25 kg (2½ lb) chicken,
   skinned and cut into 8–10
   pieces
75 g (3 oz) unsalted butter
1 tablespoon corn oil
2 onions, sliced
1 bay leaf, fresh if possible
175 ml (6 fl oz) natural yogurt
1½ teaspoons ginger pulp
1 teaspoon garlic pulp
¼ teaspoon turmeric
1 teaspoon chilli powder
¼ teaspoon ground
   cardamom
1½ teaspoons garam masala
1 teaspoon salt
3 tablespoons ground almonds
1 large red pepper, cored,
   deseeded and roughly diced
175 ml (6 fl oz) single cream
1 tablespoon chopped fresh
   coriander

ingredients

2 teaspoons coriander seeds
3 tablespoons sesame seeds
3 fresh green chillies
4 tablespoons chopped fresh coriander
2 tablespoons chopped fresh mint
3 garlic cloves, peeled
1 x 3.5 cm (1½ inch) piece fresh root ginger, shredded
1 teaspoon salt
175 ml (6 fl oz) natural yogurt
1 x 1–1.25 kg (2–2½ lb) chicken, skinned and cut into 8–10 pieces
5 tablespoons corn oil
2 onions, diced
4 green cardamoms
½ teaspoon mixed peppercorns
1 cinnamon stick
150 ml (¼ pint) water

to garnish:

2 fresh red chillies, chopped
1 teaspoon chopped fresh coriander

haandi chicken cooked in green spices and herbs

(Haandi Murgh Hara Masala)

1 Place the coriander seeds and sesame seeds in a spice grinder and grind to a paste.

2 Put the spice paste into a food processor with the green chillies, coriander, mint, garlic, half of the ginger and the salt and grind for a few seconds. Pour in the yogurt and process for 20–30 seconds. Transfer the mixture to a large mixing bowl.

3 Blend the chicken pieces with the spice mixture and set aside.

4 Heat the oil in a haandi or large saucepan and fry the onions with the cardamoms, peppercorns and cinnamon stick for 3–5 minutes.

5 Add the chicken pieces and stir-fry for about 5 minutes until well blended. Pour in the water to loosen the sauce and cook for 10–15 minutes or until the chicken is cooked and the sauce is quite thick.

6 Serve directly from the haandi, garnished with the red chillies, fresh coriander and the remaining ginger.

In this recipe, the chicken pieces are first marinated and then grilled to give them a charcoal flavour before they are added to a creamy sauce and garnished with fresh tomato. They are delicious served with Peshawari Naan (see page 111).

mughlai chicken korma

1 Place the yogurt, tomato purée, chilli powder, cumin, ground coriander, salt, lemon juice, fresh coriander and corn oil in a large mixing bowl and blend with a whisk. Add the chicken cubes, cover and leave to marinate at room temperature for about 1 hour.

2 Meanwhile, make the sauce. Whisk together the coconut milk, tomato purée, Greek yogurt, ground coriander, chilli powder, salt, ginger, garlic and the measured water. Heat the oil in a saucepan, lower the heat and add the green cardamoms and cook for about 30 seconds. Pour in the coconut mixture, stirring constantly with a wooden spoon, then stir in the sultanas, cream, fresh coriander and flaked almonds. Remove the pan from the heat and set aside.

3 Place the marinated chicken pieces on a heatproof dish and set under a preheated hot grill. Grill for about 15 minutes until thoroughly cooked, turning at least once.

4 Stir the grilled chicken pieces into the sauce and serve garnished with the sliced tomato.

ingredients
125 ml (4 fl oz) natural yogurt
1 tablespoon tomato purée
1 teaspoon chilli powder
1 teaspoon ground cumin
1 teaspoon ground coriander
1 teaspoon salt
1 tablespoon lemon juice
1 tablespoon chopped fresh coriander
1 tablespoon corn oil
500 g (1 lb) boneless, skinless chicken, cubed

sauce:
250 ml (8 fl oz) coconut milk
1 tablespoon tomato purée
2 tablespoons Greek yogurt
1 teaspoon ground coriander
1 teaspoon chilli powder
1 teaspoon salt
½ teaspoon ginger pulp
½ teaspoon garlic pulp
175 ml (6 fl oz) water
3 tablespoons corn oil
3 green cardamoms
1 tablespoon sultanas
250 ml (8 fl oz) single cream
1 tablespoon chopped fresh coriander
50 g (2 oz) flaked almonds
1 tomato, deseeded and sliced, to garnish

ingredients
4 tablespoons corn oil
4 green cardamoms
1 cinnamon stick
6 black peppercorns
4 whole cloves
2 onions, chopped
500 g (1 lb) boneless, skinless chicken, cut into 2.5 cm (1 inch) cubes
450 ml (¾ pint) water
3 fresh green chillies, chopped
2 tomatoes, quartered
2 potatoes, thickly sliced

spice paste:
2 tablespoons tomato purée
1½ teaspoons ginger pulp
1½ teaspoons garlic pulp
1½ teaspoons chilli powder
¼ teaspoon turmeric
1 teaspoon ground cumin
1½ teaspoons ground coriander
¼ teaspoon black pepper
1 teaspoon paprika
1 teaspoon sugar
1 teaspoon salt
3 tablespoons malt vinegar

Originally a Portuguese dish, vindaloos are probably best known in the West as one of the hottest curries. They are also one of the very few that contain vinegar. A great many spices are used to cook a vindaloo, so in this recipe I have tried to simplify the method of cooking as far as possible. Serve with pulao rice for a special occasion or just Plain Boiled Rice (see page 93) and Kachumer (see page 111).

chicken **vindaloo**

1 First make the spice paste, mix together all the ingredients for the paste in a medium bowl and set aside.

2 Heat the oil with the cardamoms, cinnamon, peppercorns and cloves in a medium haandi or saucepan for about 30 seconds. Add the onions and fry until golden brown. Pour in the spice mixture, reduce the heat to medium low and cook for 1–2 minutes, stirring constantly so that the mixture does not burn at the bottom.

3 Add the chicken cubes and stir-fry for 3–4 minutes.

4 Pour in the water, green chillies, tomatoes, and potatoes. Lower the heat and simmer for 12–15 minutes until the chicken and potatoes are tender. Serve hot with rice.

opposite: mughlai chicken korma

Porridge oats and four different types of lentils are used to thicken this delicious khichra, which is eaten on its own. An ideal dish for a weekday lunch party.

chicken **khichra**

(Haandi Murgh Ka Khichra)

1 Wash the dhaals thoroughly and soak overnight with the porridge oats. Drain. Place the dhaals and porridge oats in a large saucepan, add the water and boil for about 10–15 minutes until soft enough to mash. When cooked, mash to a coarse paste with a potato masher, leaving some texture in the dhaal. Set aside.

2 Place the chicken pieces in a large bowl. Stir in the yogurt, ginger, garlic, chilli powder, garam masala, turmeric, cardamoms, cinnamon and salt and mix thoroughly. Cover and set aside.

3 Heat the oil in a large saucepan or haandi and fry the onions for 3–5 minutes until golden brown. Add the chicken mixture and stir-fry, using the bhoonoing method (see page 9), for 7–10 minutes. Gradually stir in the measured water, then lower the heat and cook for about 10 minutes, stirring occasionally.

4 Remove the pan from the heat, add the mashed lentils and stir to mix thoroughly. Taste and adjust the seasoning, if necessary. If the mixture looks too thick, add about 150 ml (¼ pint) water.

5 To make the tarka, heat the ghee in a frying pan and fry the onion until crisp and golden brown.

6 While the onion is cooking, return the khichra to the heat and warm through, then transfer it to a serving dish and garnish with the chillies, fresh coriander, ginger and lemon wedges.

7 As soon as the onion is cooked, pour the seasoned ghee and onion mixture over the khichra and serve immediately.

ingredients

125 g (4 oz) chana dhaal
125 g (4 oz) masoor dhaal
125 g (4 oz) moong dhaal
125 g (4 oz) urid dhaal
75 g (3 oz) porridge oats
1.2 litres (2 pints) water

qorma:

1 x 1.5 kg (3 lb) chicken, cut into 2.5 cm (1 inch) cubes
200 ml (7 fl oz) natural yogurt
2 teaspoons ginger pulp
2 teaspoons garlic pulp
2 teaspoons chilli powder
2 teaspoons garam masala
½ teaspoon turmeric
3 green cardamoms
2 cinnamon sticks
2 teaspoons salt
6–8 tablespoons corn oil
4 onions, sliced
150 ml (¼ pint) water

tarka:

2 tablespoons ghee
1 onion, sliced

to garnish:

6 fresh green chillies, chopped
4 tablespoons chopped fresh coriander
2 x 2.5 cm (1 inch) pieces fresh root ginger, shredded
3 lemons, cut into wedges

haandi chicken
with leeks

1 Heat the corn oil with the butter in a haandi or saucepan for 1 minute, then reduce the heat and add the bay leaf. Remove from the heat.

2 Mix together the ginger, garlic, garam masala, tomato purée, salt, turmeric, chilli powder, water and sugar.

3 Return the haandi to the heat, add the spice mixture and stir-fry for about 30 seconds. Reduce the heat to medium, add the chicken pieces and leek and stir-fry for about 2 minutes, or until all the chicken pieces are well coated with the spice mixture.

4 Cover the haandi and cook for 5–7 minutes, checking occasionally that the mixture does not stick to the bottom of the haandi.

5 Finally, stir to mix, then add the green chillies and fresh coriander and cook for 2 minutes. Serve hot with Plain Boiled Rice (see page 93).

ingredients

1 tablespoon corn oil
75 g (3 oz) unsalted butter
1 large bay leaf
1 teaspoon ginger pulp
1 teaspoon garlic pulp
1 teaspoon garam masala
1 tablespoon tomato purée
1 teaspoon salt
¼ teaspoon turmeric
1 tablespoon chilli powder
1 tablespoon water
½ teaspoon sugar
500 g (1 lb) boneless, skinless chicken, cut into cubes
1 large leek, cut into 1 cm (½ inch) slices
2 fresh green chillies, diagonally sliced
1 tablespoon chopped fresh coriander

ingredients

5 tablespoons corn oil
¼ teaspoon onion seeds
4–6 curry leaves
2 onions, sliced
1½ teaspoons ginger pulp
1 teaspoon garlic pulp
1½ teaspoons chilli powder
1 teaspoon salt
2 tablespoons lemon juice
1 teaspoon dried mango powder
750 g (1½ lb) boneless, skinless chicken, cut into small pieces
600 ml (1 pint) water
250 g (8 oz) frozen French beans
3 tablespoons chopped fresh coriander
3 fresh red chillies, sliced

haandi chicken
with french beans

1 Heat the oil in a haandi or saucepan with the onion seeds and curry leaves. Add the onions and fry until golden brown.

2 Reduce the heat to low, add the ginger, garlic, chilli powder, salt, lemon juice and mango powder and stir-fry for 3–5 minutes.

3 Add the chicken pieces and stir-fry for 2 minutes.

4 Add the water and French beans and cook, covered, over a medium heat for 15–20 minutes, stirring occasionally, until the water is absorbed, then stir in the fresh coriander and red chillies.

5 Serve hot with rice or Chapati (see page 112) and a dhaal if liked.

Try and pick very small baby onions for this recipe as they look very attractive when the dish is served. I tend to prefer using small birds since they are not only quicker to cook, but also tastier.

haandi chicken
with whole fried onions

(Haandi Murgh Aur Sabuth Pyaaz)

1 Heat the oil in a haandi or saucepan, then add the baby onions, green chillies and curry leaves and fry for about 1 minute. Using a slotted spoon, remove the baby onions, chillies and curry leaves from the pan and set aside.
2 Add the diced onions to the haandi and fry for 3–5 minutes until soft and golden brown.
3 Reduce the heat to medium and add the ginger, garlic, chilli powder, ground coriander, 600 ml (1 pint) of the water and the salt. Cover the haandi with a lid and cook for 5–7 minutes until the onions are soft and the water is partly absorbed. Remove the lid, add the chicken pieces and stir-fry to coat all the chicken pieces.
4 Add the remaining water, cover with a lid and cook for 5–7 minutes until the chicken is cooked right through.
5 Remove the lid and stir-fry gently for about 5 minutes.
6 Serve hot from the haandi, garnished with fresh coriander and mint, the reserved baby onions, chillies and the curry leaves. Rice or Chapati (see page 112) go well with this dish.

ingredients
5 tablespoons corn oil
8–10 baby onions, peeled and left whole
3 whole fresh green chillies, slit in the middle
6–8 curry leaves
2 onions, finely diced
1 teaspoon ginger pulp
1 teaspoon garlic pulp
1½ teaspoons chilli powder
1 teaspoon ground coriander
750 ml (1¼ pints) water
1 teaspoon salt
1 small chicken, weighing 1 kg (2 lb) maximum, skinned and cut into 8 pieces

to garnish:
1 teaspoon chopped fresh coriander
1 teaspoon chopped fresh mint

haandi chilli-spiced chicken

(Haandi Mirch Masala Murgh)

1 Heat the oil in a haandi or saucepan over a high heat for 1 minute, then lower the heat.
2 Add the chillies and fry for about 1 minute, then remove from the pan with a slotted spoon and set aside. Add the curry leaves, onion seeds and onions and cook until the onions are golden brown.
3 While the onions are frying, mix together the tamarind pulp, brown sugar, chilli powder, ginger, garlic, cumin, ground coriander, turmeric, salt and half of the water in a small bowl to form a paste.
4 When the onions are cooked, pour in the spice mixture and stir-fry for about 2 minutes over a low heat. Stir in the chicken pieces, then add the remaining water, cover the haandi and cook for about 10–15 minutes, stirring just once or twice.
5 When the chicken is cooked, add the fresh coriander, tomato and sesame seeds and cook for 2 minutes. Serve hot with rice or a roti.

ingredients
5 tablespoons corn oil
6 large fresh green chillies, slit in the middle
4 fresh curry leaves
½ teaspoon onion seeds
2 onions, diced
2 teaspoons tamarind pulp
3 teaspoons brown sugar
1½ teaspoons chilli powder
1 teaspoon fresh ginger pulp
1 teaspoon fresh garlic pulp
1 teaspoon ground cumin
1 teaspoon ground coriander
½ teaspoons turmeric
1 teaspoon salt
300 ml (½ pint) water
1 x 1 kg (2 lb) small chicken, skinned and cut into small pieces
1 tablespoon chopped fresh coriander
1 tomato, diced
1 tablespoon sesame seeds

opposite: haandi chicken with whole fried onions

Only whole spices are used in this quick and simply prepared chicken dish. As it is a fairly dry dish, I suggest you serve Tarka Dhaal (see page 86) with it.

chicken cooked with whole spices

(Khara Masala Chicken)

1 Heat the oil in a pan and fry the onion until soft and golden brown.
2 Add the ginger, garlic, cinnamon, cardamoms, peppercorns, red and green chillies and salt and stir-fry for about 1 minute, then add the chicken pieces and stir-fry for 5–7 minutes.
3 Add the lemon juice, fresh coriander, spring onions and tomatoes and stir-fry for 3–5 minutes. Serve hot.

ingredients
4–5 tablespoons corn oil
1 large onion, sliced
1 tablespoon shredded fresh root ginger
3 garlic cloves, peeled and thickly sliced
1 cinnamon stick
2 black cardamoms
6 black peppercorns
2 fresh red chillies, sliced
1 fresh green chilli, sliced
1 teaspoon salt
500 g (1 lb) boneless, skinless chicken, cut into small pieces
1 tablespoon lemon juice
1 tablespoon chopped fresh coriander
1 bunch spring onions, roughly chopped
2 tomatoes, quartered

Spinach is one of my favourite vegetables. These days, I am pleased to say, you can buy very good quality, fresh, clean spinach at most good supermarkets. However, I also tend to use canned spinach leaves, which is not only convenient but also economical.

chicken with spinach

(Murgh Saag)

1 Heat the oil with the curry leaves in a heavy-based saucepan and fry the diced onion for 2–3 minutes over a medium heat.
2 Meanwhile, mix together the chilli powder, ginger, garlic, salt and lemon juice. Pour the mixture on to the onions, stirring constantly. Add the chicken pieces and stir-fry for about 2 minutes to seal with the spicy mixture.
3 Add the spinach and stir-fry for a further 2–3 minutes. Lower the heat and, if the mixture is very dry, add about 150 ml (¼ pint) water. Cover with a lid and cook for about 15 minutes, checking and stirring occasionally.
4 Add the red pepper, fresh coriander and green chillies and stir-fry using the bhoonoing method (see page 9), for 3–5 minutes. Serve with rice or a parata if you wish.

ingredients
5 tablespoons corn oil
4–6 curry leaves
2 onions, diced
1 teaspoon chilli powder
1½ teaspoons ginger pulp
1½ teaspoons garlic pulp
1 teaspoon salt
3 tablespoons lemon juice
500 g (1 lb) boneless, skinless chicken, cubed
425 g (14 oz) canned spinach, drained
1 red pepper, cored, deseeded and thickly sliced
2 tablespoons chopped fresh coriander
2 whole fresh green chillies, chopped

ingredients

75 g (3 oz) butter
1 tablespoon oil
1½ teaspoons garlic pulp
250 g (8 oz) boneless, skinless chicken, cut into small pieces
1 teaspoon chilli powder
1 teaspoon salt
250 g (8 oz) frozen leaf spinach, defrosted
250 g (8 oz) closed cup mushrooms, sliced
175 ml (6 fl oz) single cream
2 tablespoons chopped fresh coriander
1 teaspoon shredded root ginger, to garnish

chicken with spinach and mushrooms

1 Melt the butter with the oil in a large frying pan over a low heat. Add the garlic pulp and fry for about 30 seconds.
2 Add the chicken pieces and stir-fry for about 2 minutes, then add the chilli powder, salt, defrosted spinach and sliced mushrooms and cook for just about 7–10 minutes, stirring occasionally.
3 Stir in the cream and fresh coriander and cook for 1 minute, then transfer to a serving dish and serve garnished with the shredded ginger.

ingredients

koftas:

500 g (1 lb) boneless, skinless chicken, cubed
1 teaspoon ginger pulp
1 teaspoon garlic pulp
1½ teaspoons chilli powder
1½ teaspoons ground cumin
1½ teaspoons ground coriander
1 teaspoon salt
1 tablespoon chopped mixed fresh coriander and mint
2 large spring onions, finely chopped
2 fresh green chillies, finely chopped
1–2 tablespoons breadcrumbs
6–8 tablespoons oil, for shallow-frying

sauce:

4 tablespoons corn oil
2 onions, finely diced
2 green cardamoms
1 cinnamon stick
¼ teaspoon black cumin seeds
4 black peppercorns
1 teaspoon chilli powder
1½ teaspoons garam masala
1 teaspoon ginger pulp
1 teaspoon ground coriander
1 teaspoon garlic pulp
2 tablespoons ground almonds
250 ml (8 fl oz) coconut milk
1 teaspoon salt
150 ml (¼ pint) natural yogurt
1 tablespoon lemon juice

to garnish:

2 fresh red chillies
1 tablespoon chopped fresh coriander

These chicken koftas are easy to make and have a delicious tangy yogurt sauce. Serve them with Plain Boiled Rice (see page 93). You may be able to save time by buying the chicken already minced.

chicken koftas in a yogurt sauce

(Shorway May Murgh Kay Koftay)

1 To make the koftas, place the chicken pieces in a food processor and mince. Remove the chicken mince and set aside in a bowl.
2 Mix together the ginger, garlic, chilli powder, cumin, coriander, salt, mixed coriander and mint, spring onions and green chillies, then add the mixture to the minced chicken and mix together with your hands. Finally, work in the breadcrumbs.
3 Break off pieces about the size of a golf ball and shape into 10–12 rounds, cover and set aside.
4 Heat the oil in a large non-stick frying pan, add the koftas and cook for 1 minute on each side, turning them with a slotted spoon. Cover and set aside.
5 To make the sauce, heat the oil and fry the onions with the cardamoms, cinnamon, cumin seeds and peppercorns for 2–4 minutes over a low heat until the onions are a nice golden brown.
6 While the onions are frying, mix together the chilli powder, garam masala, ginger, ground coriander, garlic, ground almonds, coconut milk and salt. Pour the spice mixture on to the onions and stir-fry over a low heat for 3–5 minutes.
7 Beat the yogurt and add to the pan. Partially cover the pan with a lid and cook for about 2 minutes until the sauce thickens slightly. Stir in the lemon juice, then transfer the sauce to a serving dish. Reheat the koftas in a microwave for 1½ minutes or in an oven at 200°C (400°F), Gas Mark 6 for 7–10 minutes before putting them into the sauce.
8 Slit the red chillies in the middle and use to garnish the koftas, together with the fresh coriander.

spicy stir-fry chicken
haandi

(Haandi Murgh Cheat Pat)

ingredients
- 1 teaspoon garlic pulp
- 1 teaspoon ginger pulp
- 1 teaspoon chilli powder
- 1 teaspoon mango powder
- 1 teaspoon ground coriander
- 1 teaspoon salt
- ½ teaspoon brown sugar
- 2–3 tablespoons water
- 500 g (1 lb) boneless, skinless chicken, diced
- 4 tablespoons corn oil
- 4 fresh or dried curry leaves
- ½ teaspoon onion seeds
- 2–3 dried red chillies
- 2 onions, sliced
- 2 firm tomatoes, sliced
- 2 fresh green chillies
- 5–6 fresh mint leaves
- 2 tablespoons chopped fresh coriander
- 1 tablespoon lemon juice

1 In a small bowl, mix together the garlic, ginger, chilli powder, mango powder, ground coriander, salt and sugar. Pour in the measured water and mix to a paste.

2 Blend the spice mixture into the chicken pieces and set aside.

3 Heat the oil in a haandi or saucepan for 1 minute, then add the curry leaves, onion seeds and dried red chillies. Cook for 1 minute more, then add the onions and fry for 3–5 minutes until golden brown.

4 Add the chicken mixture, reduce the heat to medium and stir-fry for at least 5 minutes, reducing the heat if necessary.

5 Cover the haandi and cook for 3–5 minutes, stirring at least twice.

6 Add the tomatoes, green chillies, mint and fresh coriander, sprinkle with the lemon juice and stir-fry gently for 5–7 minutes.

7 Serve hot with Chapati (see page 112) and dhaal.

Chicken and sweetcorn always compliment each other. In this recipe, the thickly sliced grilled courgettes and peppers give the dish a crunchy barbecue flavour. Serve with Chapati or Parata (see page 112).

balti stir-fried chicken
with sweetcorn

ingredients
- 2 courgettes, thickly sliced
- 1 large red pepper, cored, deseeded and thickly sliced
- 1 tablespoon olive oil
- 4 tablespoons corn oil
- 2 onions, sliced
- 1 teaspoon ginger pulp
- 1 teaspoon chilli powder
- 1 teaspoon garlic pulp
- 1 teaspoon ground coriander
- 250 g (8 oz) boneless, skinless chicken, cut into strips
- 125 g (4 oz) sweetcorn, canned or frozen and defrosted
- 1 tablespoon lemon juice
- 2 tablespoons fresh coriander

1 Brush the courgettes and red pepper with the olive oil, then place under a preheated grill for 5–7 minutes or until they are roasted. Set aside.

2 Heat the corn oil in a balti pan, karahi or deep frying pan, then fry the sliced onions until golden brown.

3 Lower the heat and add the ginger pulp, chilli powder, garlic pulp, ground coriander and chicken strips and stir-fry for 7–10 minutes until the chicken is cooked through.

4 Add the sweetcorn, lemon juice and half of the fresh coriander and stir-fry for 2–3 minutes.

5 Finally, add the grilled vegetables and heat through. Garnish with the remaining fresh coriander and serve hot.

quick chicken and
spring onion stir-fry

1 Cook the pasta in lightly salted boiling water according to the packet instructions until just tender. Set aside.

2 Heat the butter with the oil in a saucepan. Lower the heat and add the finely diced garlic, ginger and chicken pieces and stir-fry for about 2 minutes to seal the chicken.

3 Add the pepper, turmeric, salt, Worcestershire sauce, and green and red peppers and cook for about 2 minutes, stirring occasionally.

4 Pour in the water, cover and cook over a low heat for 5 minutes. Add the spring onions, fresh coriander and cream and cook for a further 5 minutes.

5 Finally, add the cooked pasta and heat through. Serve immediately, garnished with fresh coriander.

ingredients
50 g (2 oz) small pasta twists
75 g (3 oz) butter
1 tablespoon oil
1 teaspoon finely diced garlic
1 teaspoon shredded root ginger
175 g (6 oz) boneless, skinless chicken, cut into small pieces
1 teaspoon freshly ground black pepper
¼ teaspoon turmeric
1 teaspoon salt
2 tablespoons Worcestershire sauce
½ large green pepper, cored, deseeded and thinly sliced
½ large red pepper, cored, deseeded and thinly sliced
150 ml (¼ pint) water
1 large bunch spring onions, chopped
1 tablespoon very finely chopped fresh coriander, plus extra to garnish
2 tablespoons single cream

ingredients
**250 g (8 oz) boneless, skinless
chicken breast, diced**
½ teaspoon ginger pulp
½ teaspoon garlic pulp
½ teaspoon chilli powder
½ teaspoon salt
300 ml (½ pint) water

pastry squares:
175 g (6 oz) self-raising flour
1 teaspoon salt
¼ teaspoon onion seeds
¼ teaspoon white cumin seeds
**50 g (2 oz) unsalted butter,
diced**
water, to mix
oil, for deep-frying

sweet and sour yogurt sauce:
**300 ml (½ pint) natural
yogurt**
150 ml (¼ pint) water
2 teaspoons sugar
1 teaspoon salt
**1 teaspoon crushed dried red
chillies**

sweet and sour tamarind
sauce:
2 tablespoons tamarind paste
150 ml (¼ pint) water
1 teaspoon chilli powder
1 teaspoon ground ginger
1 teaspoon sugar
1 teaspoon salt
2 tablespoons tomato sauce
1 teaspoon chopped fresh mint
**1 teaspoon chopped fresh
coriander**

to serve:
**12 baby potatoes, halved and
boiled**
**425 g (14 oz) canned
chick peas, drained**
3 shallots, cut into rings
**2 tomatoes, deseeded and
diced**
**2 fresh green chillies, chopped
(optional)**
**1 tablespoon chopped fresh
coriander**

*Chaat is probably one of the most popular snacks in India and Pakistan.
Sold at little stalls on the roadside and in bazaars, it has a sweet and sour
flavour and is usually served in little bowls with a yogurt and tamarind
topping. Although it is a vegetarian snack, I have adapted it for chicken.
This recipe can be served as a snack at any time of the day; it also makes
a very good starter.*

chicken **chaat**

1 Put the chicken pieces in a saucepan with the ginger, garlic, chilli powder,
salt and water and cook for 7–10 minutes over a medium heat until the chicken
is cooked and the water is absorbed. Set aside.
2 To make the pastry squares, sift the flour and salt into a large mixing bowl.
Add the onion seeds and cumin seeds and rub in the butter with your
fingertips. Add sufficient water to form a soft dough. Cover and leave to stand
for 10–15 minutes.
3 Roll out the dough on a lightly floured surface to a 2.5 mm (⅛ inch)
thickness. Using a pastry cutter, cut the dough into about 10 or 12 x 2.5 cm
(1 inch) squares. Set aside on a floured surface.
4 To deep-fry the squares, heat the oil in a karahi or deep frying pan over a
moderate heat and fry the squares, in batches, turning them at least twice until
they are golden brown. Remove from the pan with a slotted spoon and drain
on kitchen paper. Set aside.
5 To make the yogurt sauce, beat the yogurt with the water, sugar, salt and red
chillies. Set aside.
6 To make the tamarind sauce, put the tamarind paste into a separate bowl
with the water and beat with a whisk or a fork. Add the chilli powder, ginger,
sugar, salt, tomato sauce, mint and fresh coriander and mix thoroughly.
7 To serve, divide the chicken pieces, potatoes, chick peas and pastry squares
equally among 6 small dishes. Pour some of the yogurt sauce over each one,
then top with about 2 teaspoons of tamarind sauce. Garnish with the shallot
rings, tomatoes, green chillies, if using, and fresh coriander.

opposite: chicken chaat

ingredients
- **4 tablespoons corn oil**
- **3 onions, sliced**
- **½ teaspoon onion seeds**
- **6 curry leaves**
- **1 teaspoon ground coriander**
- **1 teaspoon garlic pulp**
- **1 teaspoon chilli powder**
- **¼ teaspoon turmeric**
- **1 teaspoon salt**
- **1 tablespoon lemon juice**
- **500 g (1 lb) boneless, skinless chicken breast, cut into small pieces**
- **2 tablespoons chopped fenugreek leaves**
- **1 large red pepper, cored, deseeded and sliced**

This light chicken stir-fry is beautifully aromatic and very easy to make. It should be served with Plain Boiled Rice (see page 93).

balti chicken
with red peppers

1 Heat the oil in a balti pan, karahi or deep frying pan and fry the onions, onion seeds and curry leaves over a medium heat for about 2 minutes.
2 Remove the pan from the heat and add the ground coriander, garlic, chilli powder, turmeric, salt, lemon juice and chicken pieces. Return the pan to the heat and stir-fry over a medium to low heat for 7–10 minutes.
3 Stir in the fenugreek and red pepper and cook for 3–5 minutes. Serve hot.

ingredients
- **750 g (1½ lb) boneless, skinless chicken, cubed**
- **1 onion, roughly sliced**
- **2 tablespoons chopped fresh mint**
- **2 tablespoons chopped fresh coriander**
- **2 fresh green chillies**
- **1 teaspoon ginger pulp**
- **1 teaspoon garlic pulp**
- **1–1½ teaspoons salt**
- **1½ teaspoons crushed coriander seeds**
- **½ teaspoon black pepper**
- **2 tablespoons breadcrumbs**
- **2 tablespoons corn oil**

These kebabs are delicious served either with a salad, or as part of a meal with a naan, a raita and a traditional Indian salad with onion rings, green chillies, lime slices, lettuce, tomatoes and cucumber. Although I have suggested you fry the kebabs, you may grill them if you prefer.

chicken seekh kebabs

1 Place the chicken pieces in a food processor and mince. Remove and set aside in a bowl.
2 Put the onion into the food processor with the mint, fresh coriander, green chillies, ginger, garlic, salt, coriander seeds and black pepper and grind for about 1 minute or until the onions are minced and all the ingredients are well blended.
3 Combine the spice mixture with the minced chicken, add the breadcrumbs and mix everything together thoroughly with your hands.
4 Break off small pieces of the mixture, a bit larger than a golf ball, and make kebabs about 5 cm (2 inches) long. If you like, you may shape them on skewers although this is not necessary.
5 Heat the oil in a non-stick pan and fry the kebabs for 1 minute, turning them gently with a slotted spoon until they are cooked through and are golden brown all over.

Although in Britain, a cutlet is generally a piece of meat with a bone, an Indian cutlet is more like a European croquette. Potato cutlets are made with a number of different fillings, such as lamb, seafood or vegetables. This particular recipe, which makes 8–10 cutlets about the size of golf balls, is quite unusual and makes a good starter served with Date and Tamarind Chutney (see page 105) or Tomato Chutney (see page 106).

potato cutlets with a spicy chicken filling

ingredients

4 large potatoes
1½ teaspoons salt
2 tablespoons chopped fresh coriander
2 fresh green chillies, chopped
2 fresh red chillies, chopped
2 tablespoons lemon juice
3 tablespoons corn oil
1 large pinch onion seeds
1 small onion, finely diced
250 g (8 oz) boneless, skinless chicken, cut into small pieces
1 teaspoon ground cumin
1½ teaspoons ground coriander
1 teaspoon garlic pulp
1 teaspoon ginger pulp
1 teaspoon chilli powder
1 teaspoon chopped mint
1 large egg, beaten
250–300 g (8–10 oz) coarse semolina
300 ml (½ pint) oil for shallow-frying

1 Boil the potatoes in lightly salted water until soft. Drain and mash, then add ½ teaspoon of the salt, 1 tablespoon fresh coriander, both the green and one of the red chillies and 1 tablespoon lemon juice and blend together. Set aside in a cool place.

2 Heat the 3 tablespoons of oil in a frying pan and fry the onion seeds and onion until golden brown. Lower the heat, add the chicken pieces and stir-fry for about 2 minutes to seal.

3 Add the cumin, ground coriander, garlic, ginger, chilli powder and remaining salt and stir-fry for 5 minutes, then stir in the remaining chillies, the remaining fresh coriander, the mint and the remaining lemon juice.

4 Remove the pan from the heat and leave to cool.

5 Using your fingers, shred the chicken pieces as finely as you can, then return to the frying pan and mix well.

6 Put the beaten egg into a shallow dish and place the semolina into a second dish. Break off 8–10 pieces of the mashed potato mixture and flatten them in the palm of your hand. Make a slight dip in the middle and fill each one with about 25 g (1 oz) of the chicken mixture. Wrap the potato around the mixture.

7 Dip the cutlets into the egg, then roll them in the semolina, coating them thoroughly. Set aside.

8 Heat the 300 ml (½ pint) oil in a frying pan and shallow-fry the cutlets, turning them frequently until golden brown.

9 Remove with a flat spoon and serve with chutney.

meat
dishes

A creamy, rich korma, which is also very fragrant as it contains saffron, cardamoms and other spices. This curry makes an excellent dinner party centrepiece, so I recommend that you use spring lamb, if available.

shahi spring lamb korma

ingredients

4 tablespoons corn oil
2 onions, finely diced
1 large bay leaf
3 green cardamoms
500 g (1 lb) spring lamb, cubed
¼ teaspoon fennel seeds
2 teaspoons coconut powder
1 teaspoon garam masala
1 teaspoon ground coriander
1 teaspoon ginger pulp
1 teaspoon chilli powder
½ teaspoon garlic pulp
1 teaspoon salt
75 ml (3 fl oz) natural yogurt
about 300 ml (½ pint) water
1 large pinch saffron
25 g (1 oz) sultanas
6–8 cashew nuts
125 ml (4 fl oz) cream
1 tablespoon chopped fresh coriander
sprig of coriander, to garnish

1 Pour the oil into a heavy-based saucepan and place over a medium heat. When the oil is hot, add the onions, bay leaf and cardamoms and fry gently until golden brown. Remove from the heat and set aside.

2 In a large mixing bowl, blend the lamb, fennel seeds, coconut powder, garam masala, ground coriander, ginger, chilli powder, garlic, salt and yogurt and mix together with your hands.

3 Return the saucepan to the heat and reheat the onion mixture for about 1 minute. Add the lamb mixture, stir with a wooden spoon to mix everything together, then cook for about 3 minutes, stirring occasionally.

4 Add the water, lower the heat, cover with a lid and cook for 20–30 minutes, checking occasionally to see if the water has evaporated.

5 When the curry looks nearly dry, check to see if the meat is tender, then add the saffron, sultanas, cashew nuts, cream and chopped fresh coriander and stir-fry for 2 minutes.

6 Transfer to a serving dish, making sure the sultanas and cashew nuts remain on top, and garnish with a sprig of fresh coriander. Serve with rice or pasta.

If you like your food hot and spicy, you will love this dish. The lamb is cut into strips, so it is more of a stir-fry than a curry. The thin strips are far easier and quicker to cook than cubes of lamb.

lamb chilli masala

(Lamb Mirch Masala)

ingredients

4–5 tablespoons corn oil
8 curry leaves
¼ teaspoon onion seeds
¼ teaspoon mustard seeds
10 baby onions
6–8 cherry tomatoes
3 onions, sliced
250 g (8 oz) lamb, cut into thin strips
1 green pepper, cored, deseeded and thickly sliced
1 red pepper, cored, deseeded and thickly sliced
1 tablespoon shredded fresh root ginger
3 garlic cloves, peeled and sliced
1½ teaspoons crushed dried red chillies
3 tablespoons lemon juice
1 teaspoon salt
1 teaspoon chopped fresh mint
1 teaspoon chopped fresh coriander
1 teaspoon coriander seeds, crushed in a pestle and mortar
1 fresh green chilli, finely chopped

1 Heat the oil in a deep frying pan, add the curry leaves, onion seeds and mustard seeds and fry for about 30 seconds, then add the baby onions and fry until they are golden brown on the outside. Remove the onions and a few of the curry leaves with a slotted spoon and set aside.

2 Add the cherry tomatoes and fry for 1 minute, then remove with a slotted spoon and place with the baby onions.

3 Reheat the oil in the frying pan, add the sliced onions and fry until golden brown. Add the lamb and stir-fry for 5–7 minutes.

4 Add half of the sliced green and red peppers, the ginger, garlic, crushed chillies, lemon juice, salt, mint and fresh coriander and stir-fry for 3–5 minutes.

5 Finally, blend in the crushed coriander seeds, green chilli, the remaining green and red peppers and the cherry tomatoes and baby onions. Serve hot with chapati (see page 112) and a dhaal.

previous page, clockwise from left: shahi spring lamb korma, tarka dhaal, plain boiled rice and lamb chilli masala

Try to choose spring lamb chops for this dish as these are far more tender and succulent than ordinary ones. Using spring lamb also cuts down on the cooking time. Serve these chops with either a salad or a rice dish and a wet dhaal such as Haandi Lentils with Lemon Juice and Fresh Tomatoes (see page 87) or Tarka Dhaal (see page 86).

lamb chops cooked in green spices

(Hara Masala Chops)

1 First make the spice paste: put the chopped fresh coriander, green chillies, lime juice, chopped mint, spring onions, garlic and salt into a food processor and grind to a fine paste.

2 Rub the spice mixture on to the lamb chops, using a fork to spread it well. Cover the chops and leave to stand for about 1 hour in a cool place.

3 Heat the oil in a large frying pan and shallow-fry the chops over a medium to low heat, three at a time, for 1½–2 minutes on each side until thoroughly cooked. Serve hot.

ingredients
12 spring lamb chops, fat removed
oil, for shallow-frying

spice paste:
6 tablespoons chopped fresh coriander
4 fresh green chillies, deseeded if wished
juice of 1 lime
1 tablespoon chopped fresh mint
6 spring onions
3 garlic cloves, peeled
1 teaspoon salt

ingredients
**2 teaspoons mixed
   peppercorns
2 teaspoons coriander seeds
½ teaspoon fennel seeds
1 teaspoon salt
1½ teaspoons ginger pulp
1 teaspoon crushed dried red
   chillies
1 tablespoon natural yogurt
3 tablespoons papaya pulp
   (see page 9)
2 tablespoons corn oil
1 kg (2 lb) lamb chops, fat
   removed**

to garnish:
**1 tablespoon chopped fresh
   coriander
4 whole fresh red chillies
10–12 onion rings**

tender lamb chops
with ginger and crushed spices

1 Grind the peppercorns, coriander seeds and fennel seeds in a spice grinder. Transfer to a bowl and add the salt, ginger, crushed dried chillies, yogurt, papaya pulp and oil. Blend together and rub the mixture over the chops.
2 Place the chops in a heatproof dish, cover with foil and leave in a cool place to marinate overnight.
3 Leave the foil over the chops and place in a preheated oven 240°C (475°F), Gas Mark 9 for 10–15 minutes, then reduce the temperature to 180°C (350°F), Gas Mark 4 and cook for a further 10 minutes.
4 Remove the foil and cook the chops for a further 7–10 minutes or until they are cooked through. Garnish with the fresh coriander, red chillies and onion rings and serve at once.

ingredients
**½ teaspoon ginger pulp
1½ teaspoons garlic pulp
1 tablespoon black pepper
2 tablespoons lemon juice
1 teaspoon salt
12 lamb chops, beaten and
   flattened with a wooden
   mallet
150 ml (¼ pint) oil, for
   shallow-frying
2 small eggs, beaten
300 g (10 oz) golden
   breadcrumbs**

to garnish:
**6–8 lettuce leaves
6–8 lime wedges
6–8 tomato wedges
1 tablespoon chopped fresh
   coriander**

The lamb chops are flattened with a wooden mallet and coated with a spicy breadcrumb mixture before they are shallow-fried. This makes a good dish for a dinner party.

lamb chops with breadcrumbs

1 Rub the ginger, garlic, black pepper, lemon juice and salt on to the chops and leave to marinate for 20–30 minutes.
2 Heat the oil in a large frying pan. Dip the chops into the beaten egg, then into the breadcrumbs and shallow-fry, three at a time, for 1½–2 minutes on each side, until thoroughly cooked.
3 Arrange the chops on a bed of lettuce and garnish with the lime and tomato wedges and chopped fresh coriander.

One of my favourite vegetables, tinday, which belongs to the squash family, is available fresh from Asian grocers, although you can also buy it in cans. In this recipe, it is combined with fresh fenugreek leaves to make a delicious and aromatic curry.

tinday with fenugreek and lamb

(Tinday Methi Aur Gosthth)

1 Heat the oil in a large saucepan, add the onions, onion seeds and curry leaves and fry for about 3 minutes. Lower the heat and add the ginger, garlic, chilli powder, turmeric, salt and lamb. Stir-fry for about 5 minutes, using the bhoonoing method (see page 9), then add the fenugreek and tinday.
2 Pour in the water and bring to the boil, stirring. Lower the heat, cover the pan and cook for 25–30 minutes, checking occasionally.
3 When the water has been absorbed, stir-fry for 5 minutes. Add the fresh coriander, tomatoes and green chillies and cook for 2 minutes to heat through. Serve with any dhaal and Plain Boiled Rice (see page 93).

ingredients
5 tablespoons corn oil
2 onions, sliced
¼ teaspoon onion seeds
6–8 curry leaves
1 teaspoon ginger pulp
1 teaspoon garlic pulp
1 teaspoon chilli powder
¼ teaspoon turmeric
1 teaspoon salt
500 g (1 lb) boned spring lamb, cut into 2.5–3.5 cm (1–1½ inch) cubes
1 small bunch fresh fenugreek
6 tinday, peeled and roughly diced
900 ml (1½ pints) water
1 tablespoon chopped fresh coriander
2 tomatoes, quartered
2 fresh green chillies, finely chopped

Doodi, a member of the squash family, and fenugreek are a very good combination and when cooked with lamb they make a delicious semi-dry curry. Serve with Haandi Lentils with Lemon Juice and Fresh Tomatoes (see page 86) and Plain Boiled Rice (see page 93).

doodi and fresh fenugreek with lamb

1 Place the lamb in a bowl and mix with the ginger, garlic, turmeric, salt and chilli powder.
2 Heat the oil in a heavy-based saucepan, add the onions and fry until golden brown. Add the lamb and fry for about 2 minutes. Add the doodi and half of the fenugreek and stir-fry for 3 minutes then pour in the water. Lower the heat and cook, covered with a lid, for 20–25 minutes or until the water has been fully absorbed and the meat is cooked.
3 Add the remaining fenugreek, the tomatoes, green pepper, lemon juice and fresh coriander and stir-fry for 7–10 minutes, or until oil begins to appear at the sides of the pan.
4 Garnish with more fresh coriander, if wished, and serve at once.

ingredients
500 g (1 lb) spring lamb, cubed
1 teaspoon ginger pulp
1 teaspoon garlic pulp
¼ teaspoon turmeric
1½ teaspoons salt
1 teaspoon chilli powder
4 tablespoons corn oil
2 onions, sliced
1 doodi, weighing about 750 g (1½ lb), peeled and roughly diced
1 handful fenugreek leaves
450 ml (¾ pint) water
2 tomatoes, quartered
1 green pepper, cored, deseeded and roughly diced
1 tablespoon lemon juice
1 tablespoon fresh coriander, plus extra to garnish (optional)

ingredients
corn oil, for deep-frying
3 potatoes, diced
500 g (1 lb) boned spring lamb, cubed
4 tablespoons natural yogurt
1 teaspoon ginger pulp
1 teaspoon chilli powder
1 teaspoon garam masala
1 teaspoon garlic pulp
⅛ teaspoon ground cardamom
1 teaspoon salt
2 onions, sliced
2 black cardamoms
¼ teaspoon black cumin seeds
1 cinnamon stick
3–4 black peppercorns
1 small bay leaf
6–8 cherry tomatoes
1 tablespoon chopped fresh coriander

Potatoes always go very well with lamb. This particular recipe which is quite a light one with a yogurt sauce could be served with either Plain Boiled Rice (see page 93) or freshly made paratas.

potatoes with lamb

(Haandi Aloo Goshth)

1 Heat the oil in a deep frying pan, add the potatoes and fry for 6–8 minutes until they are coated with the oil and a crisp golden colour. Remove from the pan with a slotted spoon and drain on kitchen paper.
2 Place the cubed lamb in a bowl, add the natural yogurt, ginger, chilli powder, garam masala, garlic, ground cardamom and salt. Rub the spices into the lamb and set aside.
3 Remove all but 5 tablespoons of oil from the pan, add the onions, cardamoms, cumin seeds, cinnamon, black peppercorns and bay leaf and fry for about 3 minutes. Add the lamb and spice mixture and stir-fry for a further 3 minutes. Cover the pan with a lid and cook for 15–20 minutes or until the liquid has evaporated and the lamb is tender.
4 Stir in the cherry tomatoes, fried potatoes and fresh coriander and heat through. Transfer to a serving dish and serve at once.

ingredients
5 tablespoons corn oil
2 onions, sliced
1 cinnamon stick
4 black peppercorns
½ teaspoon turmeric
1 teaspoon chilli powder
1 teaspoon ginger pulp
1 teaspoon garlic pulp
1 teaspoon garam masala
1 teaspoon salt
75 ml (3 fl oz) natural yogurt
500 g (1 lb) lamb, boned and diced
600 ml (1 pint) water
250 g (8 oz) plain or minted frozen peas, defrosted
1 tablespoon chopped fresh coriander
1 small red pepper, cored, deseeded and sliced

This is a delicious combination of lamb and peas. If you like the flavour of mint, use minted peas for this dish. I prefer to use leg of lamb as it is much less fatty than shoulder, but if you like shoulder I suggest you combine it with an equal quantity of leg.

haandi lamb with peas

(Haandi Matar Goshth)

1 Heat the oil in a haandi or deep saucepan and fry the onions with the cinnamon and black peppercorns until golden brown.
2 Meanwhile, mix together the turmeric, chilli powder, ginger, garlic, garam masala, salt, yogurt and lamb. Using your hands, blend everything together.
3 Turn the lamb mixture into the onions and stir-fry for 3–5 minutes using the bhoonoing method (see page 9). Pour in the water, lower the heat to medium, cover the haandi and cook for about 30 minutes, checking occasionally.
4 Once all the water has evaporated and the meat is tender, stir-fry for 2–3 minutes or until free oil appears at the sides of the pan.
5 Finally, add the peas, fresh coriander and sliced red pepper and cook gently for 2 minutes. Serve with rice and a dhaal.

opposite: potatoes with lamb

Courgettes are delicious cooked with lamb and fenugreek. Always try to choose good quality lamb, preferably spring lamb, which is not only easier to tenderize but also tastier.

lamb with courgettes and fenugreek

ingredients

5 tablespoons corn oil
2 onions, sliced
2 teaspoons ground coriander
1 pinch ground fenugreek
1 teaspoon ginger pulp
1 teaspoon garlic pulp
1 teaspoon chilli powder
1 teaspoon salt
2 tablespoons lemon juice
500 g (1 lb) boned lamb, cut into 1 cm (½ inch) cubes
5 courgettes, cut into 1 cm (½ inch) slices
1 small handful fenugreek leaves
750 ml (1¼ pints) water
2 tomatoes, quartered
1 tablespoon chopped fresh coriander
2 fresh green chillies, chopped

1 Heat the oil in a large frying pan, add the onions and fry until golden brown.
2 While the onions are cooking, blend together the ground coriander, ground fenugreek, ginger, garlic, chilli powder, salt and lemon juice. Lower the heat and stir the spice mixture into the onions. Add the lamb and half of the courgettes and fenugreek leaves and stir-fry for about 5 minutes, using the bhoonoing method (see page 9).
3 Pour in the measured water and bring to the boil, then add the remaining fenugreek leaves and courgette slices. Cook, covered, over a medium heat for about 15 minutes or until all of the water has been absorbed and the lamb is cooked through, then stir-fry for 5 minutes or until you see some free oil appearing at the sides of the pan.
4 Finally, add the tomatoes, fresh coriander and the green chillies and stir-fry for 2 minutes. Serve hot with Plain Boiled Rice (see page 93) and a lentil dish.

This is not a dish that many people cook on the Indian sub-continent, but I have always made it very successfully and it has certainly always proved very popular. It does help if the carrots are sweet as this gives the dish a sweet and sour flavour.

haandi lamb with carrots

(Haandi Gajar Goshth)

ingredients

2 carrots, peeled and cut into 1 cm (½ inch) slices
5 tablespoons corn oil
2 onions, diced
1 tomato, sliced
½ teaspoon black onion seeds
1 teaspoon ginger pulp
1 teaspoon garlic pulp
1 teaspoon chilli powder
1 teaspoon ground coriander
1 teaspoon salt
500 g (1 lb) lamb, boned and diced
750 ml (1¼ pints) water
4 mint leaves, chopped
1 tablespoon chopped fresh coriander
1 tablespoon lemon juice

1 Boil the carrot slices for about 5 minutes until soft but still firm. Drain and set them aside.
2 Heat the oil in a haandi or saucepan, add the onions and fry until golden brown. Add the sliced tomato, black onion seeds, ginger and garlic. Lower the heat and stir-fry for 2–3 minutes.
3 Add the chilli powder, ground coriander, salt and lamb to the haandi and stir-fry, using the bhoonoing method (see page 9), until the spices are well blended into the meat.
4 Pour in the water, cover the haandi or saucepan and cook for about 30 minutes, checking occasionally.
5 Once the water has been absorbed, add the carrots and stir-fry for about 5 minutes, increasing the heat if necessary.
6 Add the chopped mint, fresh coriander and lemon juice and blend together. Serve hot with Chapati (see page 112).

opposite: lamb with courgettes and fenugreek

A very versatile dish which is delicious with a fried egg and paratas for a brunch. The lamb is first simmered until tender, then stir-fried so it almost has a barbecue flavour. Sliced onions and green chillies are added towards the end and give a nice crunchy texture.

fried cubed lamb with black pepper and onions

(Kali Mirch Ka, Thala Huwa Goshth)

1 Rub the ginger, garlic, fresh coriander and salt on to the lamb and place in a saucepan. Pour in the water, add the 1 chopped chilli and bring to the boil over a medium heat. Lower the heat, partly cover the pan with a lid and cook for 15–20 minutes or until the water has almost evaporated and the lamb is tender, then stir-fry the lamb until all the water has evaporated and the meat has darkened.

2 Add the oil, then season with pepper and the fresh coriander. Add the onions and 2 roughly sliced green chillies and stir-fry for about 3–5 minutes before serving.

ingredients
- **1 teaspoon ginger pulp**
- **1 teaspoon garlic pulp**
- **2 tablespoons chopped fresh coriander**
- **1 teaspoon salt**
- **500 g (1 lb) boneless lamb, cut into small cubes**
- **300 ml (½ pint) water**
- **3 fresh green chillies, 1 chopped and 2 roughly sliced and deseeded, if wished**
- **4 tablespoons corn oil**
- **1 teaspoon freshly ground black pepper**
- **1 tablespoon chopped fresh coriander**
- **2 onions, sliced**

lamb in a spicy tangy sauce

1 Heat the oil in a saucepan and fry the chillies very quickly. Remove with a slotted spoon, drain on kitchen paper and reserve for the garnish. Add the dried onions, curry leaves and onion seeds and fry over a medium heat for 3–5 minutes.

2 Add the lamb, ginger and garlic and stir-fry for 2 minutes over a low heat. Meanwhile, mix together the chilli powder, salt, ground coriander, cumin, tamarind paste, tomato purée, sugar and 150 ml (¼ pint) of the water. Pour the spice mixture on to the lamb, increase the heat to medium and cook until the mixture boils.

3 Pour in the remaining 600 ml (1 pint) water, lower the heat slightly, cover the pan with a lid and cook for 25–30 minutes, checking occasionally. Once all the water has been absorbed, stir-fry with a wooden spoon for about 2 minutes or until oil begins to appear at the sides of the pan.

4 To serve, sprinkle the sesame seeds over the lamb and garnish with the fresh coriander and the fried green chillies.

ingredients
- **6 tablespoons corn oil**
- **4 large fresh green chillies, slit and deseeded**
- **2 dried onions**
- **6 curry leaves**
- **¼ teaspoon onion seeds**
- **500 g (1 lb) lamb, cubed**
- **1 teaspoon ginger pulp**
- **1 teaspoon garlic pulp**
- **1 teaspoon chilli powder**
- **1 teaspoon salt**
- **1½ teaspoons ground coriander**
- **1 teaspoon ground cumin**
- **1 tablespoon tamarind paste**
- **1 tablespoon tomato purée**
- **½ teaspoon sugar**
- **750 ml (1¼ pints) water**

to garnish:
- **1 teaspoon sesame seeds**
- **2 tablespoons chopped fresh coriander**

ingredients

1 kg (2 lb) lean lamb, boned and cubed
2 teaspoons ginger pulp
2 teaspoons garlic pulp
2 teaspoons ground coriander
1 teaspoon ground cumin
1½ teaspoons chilli powder
1½ teaspoons salt
4 tablespoons natural yogurt
2 tablespoons papaya pulp (see page 9)

salad garnish:

4 tablespoons corn oil
12–14 cherry tomatoes
12–14 shallots, peeled
1 red onion, cut into rings
6–8 iceberg lettuce leaves
2 fresh green chillies, sliced
2 fresh red chillies, sliced
2 tablespoons chopped mixed fresh mint and coriander
1 bunch watercress
2 limes, quartered

This is a delicious way of serving cubed lamb and a very popular one, especially in Pakistan where it is barbecued in the open at many restaurants. Serve these kebabs as a starter or as part of a barbecue. Raw papaya, which is probably the best tenderizer available, is used to tenderize the lamb. Serve with a raita.

spiced **cubes of lamb**

(Boti Kebabs)

1 Place the lamb, ginger, garlic, ground coriander, cumin, chilli powder, salt and natural yogurt in a large mixing bowl and mix together with your fingers. Add the papaya pulp and rub the spice mixture into the meat. Cover and set aside for at least 4 hours at room temperature.

2 Io make the salad garnish, heat the oil in a deep frying pan and fry the cherry tomatoes and shallots very quickly so they just darken on the outside. Remove with a slotted spoon and arrange on a serving dish with the onion rings, lettuce leaves, green and red chillies and set aside.

3 Place the lamb in a roasting tin and cook in a preheated oven, 190°C (375°F), Gas Mark 5, for 25–30 minutes, checking and basting with the oil from the frying pan at least twice. Transfer the lamb cubes to the serving dish, sprinkle with the mint and fresh coriander and arrange the watercress and lime quarters around the edge.

This is a traditional recipe which is made for weddings and other special occasions. It can also be made with minced beef but, whether using lamb or beef a lean mince is preferable.

baked lamb kheema
(Dum Ka Qeema)

ingredients
**2 tablespoons papaya pulp
  (see page 9)
750 g (1½ lb) minced lamb
3 tablespoons natural yogurt
1 teaspoon chilli powder
½ teaspoon ginger pulp
1½ teaspoons garlic pulp
1 teaspoon salt
1½ teaspoons garam masala
1 teaspoon ground allspice
2 fresh green chillies
3 tablespoons chopped fresh
  coriander
5 tablespoons corn oil
3 onions, very finely diced**

to garnish:
**1 red onion, cut into rings
1 tablespoon chopped fresh
  coriander
1 lemon, cut into wedges
1 tablespoon chopped fresh
  mint**

1 Place the papaya pulp in a bowl, add the minced lamb, yogurt, chilli powder, ginger, garlic, salt, garam masala and allspice and mix together well with your hands. Put the green chillies and fresh coriander in a food processor and grind for about 1 minute, then add to the minced lamb. Cover and set aside for about 1 hour.
2 Meanwhile, heat the oil in a saucepan and fry the onions until golden brown. Set aside.
3 Place the spicy lamb mixture in a food processor and grind for 1 minute to make the mixture finer and more of a paste. Add to the onions and mix well. Return the pan to the heat and stir-fry for about 2 minutes, to seal.
4 Transfer the lamb mixture to an ovenproof dish and bake in a preheated oven, 190°C (375°F), Gas Mark 5, for about 20 minutes, checking and stirring at least once.
5 Serve garnished with the onion rings, coriander, lemon wedges and mint.

haandi minced lamb with whole spices
(Haandi Qeema Loijh Khara Masala)

ingredients
**4 tablespoons corn oil
2 onions, finely sliced
1 x 3.5 cm (1½ inch) piece of
  fresh root ginger, peeled and
  shredded
2 garlic cloves, roughly sliced
2 dried chillies, crushed
½ teaspoon salt
1 cinnamon stick
2 large black cardamoms
3 black peppercorns
750 g (1½ lb) minced lamb**

to serve:
**1 fresh green chilli, sliced
2 tablespoons finely chopped
  fresh coriander
2 tomatoes, quartered**

1 Heat the oil in a haandi or deep saucepan and fry the onions until golden brown.
2 While the onions are cooking, mix together the shredded ginger, garlic, chillies and salt. Pour the mixture into the fried onions, then add the cinnamon, cardamoms and peppercorns. Lower the heat and stir-fry for 2–3 minutes.
3 Add the minced lamb and continue stir-frying for 7–10 minutes until oil appears on the sides of the haandi, breaking up any lumps with a masher.
4 Finally, add the green chilli, fresh coriander and tomatoes and heat through, stirring constantly. Serve hot with Chapati (see page 112).

opposite: baked lamb kheema

Shaami kebabs are made with minced or cubed lamb and cooked with spices and a binding agent before being made into kebabs. There are several ways of making shaami kebabs, in fact, each household may have a different recipe. This particular recipe has been handed down to me by my mother and over the years it has become a great favourite amongst my friends. Serve with a lentil dish such as Tarka Dhaal (see page 86), or with any wet vegetable curry with a raita and rice.

shaami kebabs

ingredients

2 tablespoons chana dhaal
1.5 litres (2½ pints) water
500 g (1 lb) lean lamb, boned and cubed
1 teaspoon ginger pulp
1 teaspoon garlic pulp
1½ teaspoons chilli powder
1½ teaspoons salt
1 teaspoon garam masala
1 tablespoon ground almonds
4 fresh green chillies, chopped
6 tablespoons chopped fresh coriander (2 tablespoons very finely chopped)
4 tablespoons corn oil
1 onion, sliced
2 tablespoons natural yogurt
1 egg
1 green chilli, very finely chopped
4–5 tablespoons oil, for shallow-frying

1 Wash the chana dhaal thoroughly, place in a heavy-based saucepan with 600 ml (1 pint) water and cook over a medium heat for 15–20 minutes until the water has been fully absorbed and the chana dhaal is soft enough to be mashed to a paste. Use a food processor to do this if you like.

2 Mix together the lamb, ginger, garlic, chilli powder, salt, garam masala, ground almonds, green chillies and 4 tablespoons fresh coriander.

3 Heat the oil in a saucepan, add the onion and fry until golden brown. Add the spiced lamb and turn to seal the juices. Pour in 900 ml (1½ pints) water and lower the heat. Cover with a lid and cook until the water has been fully absorbed and the lamb is soft enough to be ground in a food processor. However, it is important not to grind the lamb too much as this spoils the texture of the kebabs, so just grind for about 1½ minutes. Transfer the ground lamb to a bowl.

4 Pour in the yogurt and the chana dhaal paste and mix in well with your hands. Beat the egg and add to the lamb. Finally, add the remaining very finely chopped fresh coriander and the chopped green chilli. Break off pieces of the lamb mixture and make about 12 flat rounds in the palms of your hands.

5 Heat the oil in a frying pan and gently drop in 2 kebabs at a time and fry for 2–3 minutes, turning once. Drain on kitchen paper. Serve hot.

Always use good lean minced lamb which will not have such a fatty taste and, ideally, try to buy aubergines from an Asian grocer as they are smaller, tastier and do not contain as much water as those available from large supermarkets.

ingredients

5 tablespoons corn oil
2 onions, sliced
6–8 curry leaves
500 g (1 lb) minced lamb
1 teaspoon ginger pulp
1 teaspoon garlic pulp
1 teaspoon chilli powder
¼ teaspoon turmeric
1 teaspoon ground coriander
1 teaspoon salt
4 small or 2 medium aubergines, trimmed and cut into 2.5–3.5 cm (1–1½ inch) pieces
3 fresh red chillies, slit in the middle and deseeded
2 tablespoons chopped fresh coriander

aubergines with minced lamb

(Haandi Baigun Qeema)

1 Heat the oil in a haandi or a saucepan and fry the onions and curry leaves for 3–5 minutes until golden brown.
2 While the onions are frying, mix together the minced lamb, ginger, garlic, chilli powder, turmeric, ground coriander and salt. When the onions are a soft golden brown, add the minced lamb and stir-fry for about 5–7 minutes using the bhoonoing method (see page 9).
3 Add the aubergines and stir-fry for about 3–5 minutes until the lamb and aubergines are cooked.
4 Add the red chillies and fresh coriander and stir-fry for 3–5 minutes. Serve hot with rice or Chapati (see page 112).

I recommend you use fresh spinach leaves for this recipe. However, if unavailable, you can use frozen or canned spinach. As always, a lean mince is preferable.

ingredients

1 kg (2 lb) fresh spinach leaves
4 tablespoons corn oil
2 onions, sliced
1 cinnamon stick
3 black cardamoms
4 black peppercorns
500 g (1 lb) minced lamb
1 teaspoon salt
1 teaspoon garam masala
1 teaspoon ginger pulp
1 teaspoon garlic pulp
1 teaspoon chilli powder
1 green pepper, cored, deseeded and sliced
2 tomatoes, quartered
1 tablespoon chopped fresh coriander

spinach with minced lamb

(Haandi Saag Qeema)

1 Wash the spinach leaves thoroughly and cook in the water left on the leaves. Drain, squeeze out any excess water and set aside.
2 Heat the oil in a haandi or heavy-based saucepan and fry the onions with the cinnamon stick, cardamoms and black peppercorns for 5 minutes.
3 Put the lamb into a bowl, add the salt, garam masala, ginger, garlic and chilli powder and mix well. Add the lamb mixture to the onions, lower the heat to medium and stir-fry for about 5 minutes using the bhoonoing method (see page 9).
4 Add the drained spinach and stir it well into the mince. Add the green pepper and tomatoes and stir-fry for 7–10 minutes.
5 Finally, add the fresh coriander and stir-fry for 2–3 minutes. Serve with rice or Paratas (see page 112).

Potato and cauliflower are a delicious combination. In this recipe, the spicy minced lamb is fried separately and mixed together with the cooked vegetables just before serving.

balti fried potatoes and cauliflower with minced lamb

(Aloo Gobi Aur Qeema)

ingredients
7 tablespoons corn oil
4–6 curry leaves
½ teaspoon onion seeds
2 potatoes, diced
250 g (8 oz) cauliflower, cut into small florets
1 red pepper, cored, deseeded and sliced
½ teaspoon salt
2 onions, sliced
1 teaspoon ginger pulp
1 teaspoon garlic pulp
¼ teaspoon turmeric
1½ teaspoons chilli powder
1 teaspoon salt
500 g (1 lb) lean minced lamb
2 tablespoons chopped fresh coriander

1 Heat 3 tablespoons of the oil in a frying pan, add the curry leaves and onion seeds and fry for about 30 seconds. Add the potato and cauliflower florets and cook for 2 minutes, then add the red pepper and sprinkle with the salt. Turn the heat to very low, cover the pan and let the vegetables steam lightly for 5–7 minutes. Turn the heat off once the potatoes are cooked.
2 Heat the remaining oil in a balti pan, karahi or a deep frying pan and fry the onions for 5 minutes, then lower the heat and add the ginger, garlic, turmeric, chilli powder, salt, and minced lamb. Stir-fry, using the bhoonoing method (see page 9), for 10 minutes, breaking up any lumps that form, using a potato masher if necessary. Stir in the fresh coriander, then remove from heat.
3 With a slotted spoon remove all the vegetables from the frying pan and place them on top of the lamb. Reheat, gently mixing the lamb and vegetables before serving.

Fresh fenugreek can be very aromatic. This particular recipe is a very simple one – as a child I remember it was a family favourite and always went down well.

haandi minced lamb with fenugreek

(Bhoono Haandi Cleema Methi)

1 Heat the oil in a haandi or suacepan for about 2 minutes, add the onions and curry leaves and cook for about 3–5 minutes over a medium heat. Add 1 of the tomatoes, the garlic, ginger, chilli powder and salt and stir to mix.
2 Add the minced lamb and fenugreek leaves and stir-fry for 7–10 minutes using the bhoonoing method (see page 9). If lumps of mince begin to form, break them up with a masher.
3 Finally, stir in the red chillies, the remaining tomato and the fresh coriander. Serve hot with rice and a dhaal.

ingredients
4 tablespoons corn oil
2 onions, sliced
4 fresh curry leaves
2 tomatoes, sliced
1 teaspoon garlic pulp
1 teaspoon ginger pulp
1 teaspoon chilli powder
1 teaspoon salt
500 g (1 lb) minced lamb
leaves from 1 large bunch fresh fenugreek
2 fresh red chillies, chopped
3 tablespoons chopped fresh coriander

opposite: balti fried potatoes and cauliflower with minced lamb

This recipe, which makes 10–12 kebabs, originated in Peshawar, in northern Pakistan. Ground pomegranate seeds are used, giving the kebabs a delicious tangy flavour. Serve them either as part of a meal, in a burger bun as a snack, or with a salad as a starter.

minced lamb kebabs

(Chaplee Kebab, Peshawari)

1 Put the minced lamb into a food processor and grind for 1 minute to make it even finer. Transfer to a bowl and add the spring onions, tomatoes, fresh coriander, green chillies, red chillies, peppercorns, coriander seeds, garlic, ginger, salt and ground pomegranate seeds and mix together with your fingers.
2 Add the flour and egg and mix thoroughly. Break off small pieces of the mixture and flatten them in the palm of one hand, using the fingers of the other hand to pat them flat.
3 Heat sufficient oil to shallow-fry the kebabs in a large heavy-based frying pan and fry, 2 at a time, pressing them down with a slotted spoon. Serve hot.

ingredients
500 g (1 lb) minced lamb
6 spring onions, chopped
2 tomatoes, skinned, deseeded and diced
2 tablespoons chopped fresh coriander
1–2 fresh green chillies, finely chopped
½ teaspoon crushed dried red chillies
6 black peppercorns, crushed
1 teaspoon coriander seeds, crushed in a pestle and mortar
1 teaspoon garlic pulp
1 teaspoon ginger pulp
1 teaspoon salt
1½ teaspoons ground pomegranate seeds
1 tablespoon plain flour
1 egg, beaten
6–8 tablespoons oil, for shallow-frying

lamb koftas with potatoes

1 Heat the oil in a deep frying pan and fry the baby potatoes over a medium heat until golden brown and fully cooked. Lift out with a slotted spoon and drain on kitchen paper. Set aside.
2 Place the lamb in a food processor and grind for about 40–50 seconds to make it even finer. Transfer to a bowl and add the onion, green chillies, fresh coriander, garam masala, chilli powder, ginger, poppy seeds, garlic and salt. Using your fingers, mix the spices into the minced lamb. Add the beaten egg and blend in. Break off small pieces of the lamb mixture, each about the size of a golf ball and shape into balls.
3 Reheat the oil in the frying pan and fry all the koftas for about 2–2½ minutes each over a medium heat until cooked through. Lift out with a slotted spoon and drain on kitchen paper. Set aside.
4 To make the sauce, heat the oil and fry the onions for 5–7 minutes until crispy and golden brown. Lift them out with a slotted spoon and drain on kitchen paper. Leave to cool.
5 When the onions have cooled, grind them in a food processor, then return them to the oil and fry with the bay leaf and green cardamoms for 30 seconds. Add the tomato purée, garam masala, ginger, garlic, chilli powder, ground coriander and salt, stirring constantly. Beat the yogurt, pour in and continue stirring over a medium heat.
6 Add the koftas one by one, then add the potatoes, partially cover the saucepan and cook for 5–7 minutes. If you feel the sauce is too thick, add a little water.
7 Garnish with the fresh coriander and mint and serve hot.

ingredients
corn oil, for deep-frying
12 baby potatoes, halved
500 g (1 lb) minced lamb
1 onion, finely diced
2 fresh green chillies, chopped
2 tablespoons finely chopped fresh coriander
1½ teaspoons garam masala
1 teaspoon chilli powder
1 teaspoon ginger pulp
2 teaspoons white poppy seeds
1 teaspoon garlic pulp
1 teaspoon salt
1 small egg, beaten

sauce:
4 tablespoons corn oil
onions, diced
1 bay leaf
3 green cardamoms
1 tablespoon tomato purée
1 teaspoon garam masala
1 teaspoon ginger pulp
1 teaspoon garlic pulp
1 teaspoon chilli powder
2 teaspoons ground coriander
1 teaspoon salt
3 tablespoons natural yogurt

to garnish:
2 tablespoons chopped fresh coriander
2 tablespoons chopped fresh mint

If you can, make these pasties in large quantities as they freeze very well. They can be served as a starter with a salad, or as a snack at any time of the day; and they are also excellent for picnics. Although I have given a recipe for rough puff pastry, the ready-made frozen variety is perfectly suitable for this recipe.

spicy minced beef pasties

1 Place the minced beef in a food processor and grind it for about 1 minute to make it even finer.
2 Heat the oil in a saucepan, add the onions and curry leaves and fry for about 2 minutes. Lower the heat and add the ginger, chilli powder, garlic, garam masala, salt and green chilli. Stir in the mince and stir-fry very quickly for about 5 minutes, using a potato masher to prevent any lumps forming.
3 Finally, add the fresh coriander and stir-fry for 3–5 minutes. Remove from the heat and set aside to cool.
4 To make the rough puff pastry, sift the flour and salt into a large mixing bowl. Cut the butter into small cubes and drop them on to the flour, covering them fully with the flour. Gradually stir in the water, mixing to form a soft dough. Cover and set aside in a cool place for about 15 minutes.
5 Roll out the pastry on a lightly floured board. Then fold the pastry in half, roll it out again, then repeat the process once more so that you end up with 2–3 layers.
6 Break off small pieces of dough and roll them into rounds about 10–12 cm (4–5 inches) in diameter, put a tablespoonful of the beef mixture on to one half of each round. Dampen the edges of each round lightly with water, then fold over each pastry and brush with beaten egg.
7 Place the pasties on a baking tray and bake in a preheated oven, 180°C (350°F), Gas Mark 4, for 15–20 minutes.

ingredients
500 g (1 lb) lean minced beef
4 tablespoons corn oil
2 onions, diced
4–6 curry leaves
1 teaspoon ginger pulp
1½ teaspoons chilli powder
1 teaspoon garlic pulp
1 teaspoon garam masala
1 teaspoon salt
1 fresh green chilli, deseeded and diced
1 tablespoon chopped fresh coriander

rough puff pastry:
275 g (9 oz) plain flour
½ teaspoon salt
175 g (6 oz) butter
150 ml (¼ pint) water
beaten egg, to glaze

spicy minced beef with pasta and peppers

1 Cook the pasta twists in a saucepan of lightly salted boiling water according to the packet instructions.
2 Meanwhile, heat the corn oil in a large frying pan, add the onions and fry until soft and golden brown. Add the ginger, garlic, chilli powder, turmeric and ground coriander and cook for 1 minute.
3 Add the minced beef and stir-fry using the bhoonoing method (see page 9), for 5–7 minutes. Add the peppers and stir-fry for 3–5 minutes. Add the fresh coriander and stir it into the beef. Finally, drain the pasta well and stir it in to the beef over a high heat to warm through.

ingredients
50 g (2 oz) pasta twists
5 tablespoons corn oil
2 onions, chopped
1½ teaspoons ginger pulp
1½ teaspoons garlic pulp
1 teaspoon chilli powder
¼ teaspoon turmeric
1 teaspoon ground coriander
500 g (1 lb) minced beef
1 green pepper, cored, deseeded and sliced
1 yellow pepper, cored, deseeded and sliced
2 tablespoons chopped fresh coriander

fish and seafood

ingredients
1 tablespoon tomato purée
175 ml (6 fl oz) coconut milk
2 tablespoons ground almonds
1 teaspoon ginger pulp
1 teaspoon garlic pulp
1 teaspoon chilli powder
**¼ teaspoon ground
  cardamom**
1 teaspoon garam masala
4 tablespoons corn oil
**12–15 frozen cooked king
  prawns, defrosted and
  peeled**
**1 tablespoon chopped fresh
  coriander**
**1 small green pepper, cored,
  deseeded and thinly sliced**
**125–150 ml (4–5 fl oz) single
  cream**
**sprig of fresh coriander, to
  garnish**

*This is a fairly mild dish made with coconut milk. It has a nice thick sauce
and can be eaten with plain fried rice. Although I have used king prawns,
you may use smaller ones if you prefer.*

king prawn korma

1 In a bowl, mix together the tomato purée, coconut milk, ground almonds,
ginger, garlic, chilli powder, ground cardamom and garam masala.
2 Heat the oil in a heavy-based saucepan, pour in the coconut mixture and
stir-fry over a medium heat for about 2 minutes. Add the king prawns and stir-
fry for 5 minutes.
3 Add the fresh coriander, green pepper and cream and bring to the boil.
Transfer to a serving dish and garnish with a sprig of coriander.

ingredients
4 tablespoons corn oil
¼ teaspoon mustard seeds
8–10 curry leaves
6 whole dried red chillies
2 garlic cloves
**15 frozen cooked king prawns,
  defrosted and peeled**
**2 tablespoons chopped fresh
  coriander**

coconut sauce:
250 ml (8 fl oz) coconut milk
300 ml (½ pint) water
1 teaspoon ginger pulp
1 teaspoon garlic pulp
1 teaspoon chilli powder
1 teaspoon salt
1½ teaspoons tomato purée

king prawn masala
in a creamy coconut sauce

1 First, prepare the coconut sauce. Mix together the coconut milk, water,
ginger, garlic, chilli powder, salt and tomato purée in a bowl. Cover and leave
to stand for 20 minutes.
2 Heat the oil in a deep frying pan with the mustard seeds, curry leaves, dried
red chillies and garlic cloves and fry for about 30 seconds. Lower the heat,
add the prawns and quickly stir-fry for about 2 minutes, stirring continuously.
3 Pour in the coconut sauce and cook for about 5 minutes. Add half of the
fresh coriander and stir to mix. Transfer to a serving dish and serve garnished
with the remaining fresh coriander.

opposite: king prawn korma

ingredients
4 tablespoons corn oil
¼ teaspoon onion seeds
4 curry leaves
2 onions, sliced
1 teaspoon ginger pulp
1 teaspoon garlic pulp
½ teaspoon ground coriander
1 teaspoon chilli powder
¼ teaspoon turmeric
1 teaspoon salt
2 tablespoons lemon juice
250 g (8 oz) frozen cooked prawns, defrosted and peeled
1 x 425 g (14 oz) can chick peas, drained
1 tablespoon chopped fresh coriander
2 slices red pepper, diced

This recipe involves a delicious and unusual combination of prawns and chick peas. I find that canned chick peas have the ideal texture for this dish and also save time.

prawns with chick peas

1 Heat the corn oil in a frying pan with the onion seeds, curry leaves and onions for about 5 minutes over a medium heat. Lower the heat and add the ginger, garlic, ground coriander, chilli powder, turmeric and salt and mix together. Pour in the lemon juice.
2 Add the prawns and stir-fry for about 5 minutes. Add the chick peas and cook for about 7–10 minutes, stirring occasionally.
3 When the prawns are cooked and the chick peas have absorbed all the flavours, stir in the fresh coriander and diced red pepper.
4 Serve hot with chapati (see page 112).

ingredients
75 g (3 oz) butter
1 tablespoon corn oil
3 garlic cloves, sliced
1 tablespoon shredded fresh root ginger
2 bunches spring onions, chopped
1 teaspoon chilli powder
1 teaspoon salt
250 g (8 oz) monkfish, cubed
8–10 fresh or frozen cooked king prawns, peeled, fresh or frozen
75 g (3 oz) mushrooms, thickly sliced
½ green pepper, cored, deseeded and sliced
½ red pepper, cored, deseeded and sliced
4 tablespoons single cream
1 tablespoon finely chopped fresh coriander

Ready-prepared fresh fish is available at most supermarkets these days, making it much easier to cook fish without having to spend a lot of time preparing and cleaning it. Monkfish is a very simple fish to cook as it does not break up, making it ideal for stir-frying.

fried monkfish and prawns with mushrooms

1 Heat the butter and corn oil in a large frying pan over a medium heat. Add the garlic, ginger, spring onions, chilli powder and salt and stir-fry for about 1 minute, then add the monkfish and prawns and stir-fry for 5–7 minutes over a medium heat.
2 Add the mushrooms and stir-fry for 3–5 minutes. Finally, add the peppers, cream and fresh coriander and cook for 2 minutes.

opposite: fried monkfish and prawns with mushrooms

ingredients

6 plaice fillets
2 tablespoons lemon juice
1 tablespoon tomato purée
1 teaspoon ginger pulp
1 teaspoon garlic pulp
1 teaspoon chilli powder
2 teaspoons ground coriander
1 teaspoon ground cumin
1 teaspoon salt
3–4 tablespoons water
2 tablespoons corn oil

to garnish:

**2 tablespoons chopped fresh
    coriander**
lemon wedges

*'Tandoori' is a method of cooking which takes its name from the special
cylindrical clay oven called a tandoor, originally used on a bed of embers
to ensure the flesh of the chicken or fish is tender and the outside crispy.
I have suggested plaice fillets for this recipe, although halibut and cod are
also suitable.*

tandoori **fish**

1 Wash the plaice fillets and pat them dry with kitchen paper. Rub them with
the lemon juice and set aside.
2 In a bowl, blend the tomato purée with the ginger, garlic, chilli powder,
ground coriander, ground cumin, salt, water and oil. Pour the mixture over the
plaice fillets, cover and leave to marinate in a cool place for about 2 hours.
3 Place the fillets under a preheated medium grill and cook for 7–10 minutes
or until brown patches begin to appear on the top. Garnish with fresh
coriander and lemon wedges and serve with naan bread.

ingredients

1 teaspoon ground cumin
2 teaspoons ground coriander
2 teaspoons ginger pulp
2 teaspoons garlic pulp
2½ teaspoons chilli powder
2 teaspoons mango powder
2 teaspoons salt
2 tablespoons lemon juice
500 g (1 lb) cod fillet, cubed
2 tablespoons cornflour
**300 ml (½ pint) corn oil, for
    deep-frying, plus an extra
    3–4 tablespoons, for
    shallow-frying**
½ teaspoon mustard seeds
4–6 curry leaves
4 onions, sliced
¼ teaspoon turmeric
**1 red pepper, cored, deseeded
    and thinly sliced**
**1 green pepper, cored,
    deseeded and thinly sliced**

haandi fish dopiaza

1 In a large bowl, mix together the ground cumin, 1 teaspoon each of the
ground coriander, ginger and garlic, 1½ teaspoons of the chilli powder, the
mango powder, 1 teaspoon salt and the lemon juice. Drop the pieces of cod
into the spice mixture and coat them thoroughly. Sprinkle the cornflour on top
and shake the bowl a few times to coat the cod with the cornflour.
2 Heat the oil for deep-frying in a deep frying pan, add the fish pieces a few
at a time and fry for 1½–2 minutes, stirring gently with a slotted spoon. Transfer
the cod to a heatproof dish, cover and keep warm in a low oven.
3 Heat 3–4 tablespoons oil in a haandi or a heavy-based saucepan, add the
mustard seeds, curry leaves and onions and fry until soft and golden brown.
Lower the heat and add the turmeric and the remaining ginger, garlic, chilli
powder, salt and ground coriander and stir-fry for 3–5 minutes.
4 Remove the fish from the oven and add to the onion mixture. Stir in the sliced
red and green peppers and stir-fry for 2 minutes. Serve directly from the
haandi if wished.

opposite: haandi fish dopiaza

vegetable dishes

haandi chana dhaal with
tomatoes and green mango slices

(Chanay Ki Dhaal Tamatar Aur Kairi)

1 Wash the chana dhaal thoroughly. Boil for about 10 minutes until soft but not mushy, drain, then set aside.
2 Heat the oil in a haandi or saucepan and fry the onion seeds and curry leaves for about 2 minutes.
3 Meanwhile, put the spring onions into a bowl. Mix together the ginger, garlic, ground coriander, cumin, chilli powder and salt. Stir this spice mixture into the spring onions, then lower the heat on the stove, add the spring onion mixture to the haandi and stir-fry for about 2 minutes. Add the mango slices and chana dhaal and blend together.
4 Finally, add the tomatoes, green chillies and the mixed mint and coriander and stir everything together. Serve immediately.

ingredients
300 g (10 oz) chana dhaal
4 tablespoons corn oil
¼ teaspoon onion seeds
4–6 curry leaves
2 large bunches spring onions, including most of the green part, finely chopped
1 teaspoon ginger pulp
1 teaspoon garlic pulp
1 teaspoon ground coriander
1 teaspoon ground cumin
1 teaspoon chilli powder
1½ teaspoons salt
1 unripe green mango, peeled, stoned and roughly sliced
2 tomatoes, sliced
3 whole fresh green chillies
2 tablespoons chopped mixed fresh mint and coriander

Baby aubergines are available at Asian grocers and are full of flavour. They look very attractive at the dinner table and make a good extra dish. Slit the chillies in the middle and remove the seeds if you do not want the dish to be too hot.

whole baby aubergines
with red chillies

1 Heat the oil in a saucepan, add the onion with the curry leaves, onion seeds, garlic, ginger and chilli powder and fry for about 1½ minutes.
2 Drop in the baby aubergines and red chillies and lower the heat. Add the lemon juice, salt and fenugreek and stir to mix. Cover the saucepan with a lid, lower the heat further and cook for 7–10 minutes, checking at least once and stirring gently if required.
3 Add the cherry tomatoes and chopped fresh coriander and cook for a further 2 minutes before serving.

ingredients
5 tablespoons corn oil
1 onion, sliced
4–6 curry leaves
¼ teaspoon onion seeds
4 garlic cloves, halved
1 tablespoon shredded fresh root ginger
1 teaspoon chilli powder
8–10 baby aubergines, trimmed and slit lengthways
8 fresh red chillies, slit and deseeded
1 tablespoon lemon juice
1 teaspoon salt
2 tablespoons chopped fenugreek
6 cherry tomatoes
1 tablespoon chopped fresh coriander

previous page, clockwise from left: haandi chana dhaal with tomatoes and green mango slices, natural yogurt and whole baby aubergines with red chillies

ingredients

2 red peppers
2 green peppers
75 g (3 oz) butter
2 onions, finely diced
¼ teaspoon onion seeds
4 curry leaves
2 large carrots, diced
50 g (2 oz) frozen peas,
   defrosted
50 g (2 oz) canned broad
   beans, drained
2 potatoes, diced
50 g (2 oz) sultanas
10 cashew nuts
1 teaspoon ground coriander
1 teaspoon garlic pulp
1 teaspoon crushed dried
   red chillies
125 g (4 oz) long-grain rice,
   cooked
1 teaspoon salt

Shimla mirch is another name for red or green peppers. In this recipe, which makes an impressive dinner party centrepiece, they are baked, stuffed with a mixture of rice, vegetables and sultanas. It is important to dice the vegetables very finely as they are only very quickly stir-fried.

baked **shimla mirch**

1 Gently remove the tops of the peppers. Scrape out the seeds and ribs and sit the peppers in an ovenproof dish.
2 Melt the butter in a medium frying pan, add the onions, onion seeds, curry leaves, carrots, peas, broad beans, potatoes, sultanas, cashew nuts, ground coriander, garlic and red chillies and quickly stir-fry for about 5 minutes. Add the cooked rice and stir-fry for 2–3 minutes. Sprinkle with the salt, stir it in and divide the mixture equally among the peppers. Replace the tops.
3 Place the peppers in a preheated oven, 180°C (350°F), Gas Mark 4, for 12–15 minutes. Serve immediately.

ingredients

50 g (2 oz) tamarind
600 ml (1 pint) hot water
3 tablespoons sesame seeds
2 tablespoons desiccated
   coconut
2 teaspoons ground coriander
2 teaspoons ground cumin
1½ teaspoons ginger pulp
1½ teaspoons garlic pulp
1 teaspoon salt
¼ teaspoon turmeric
2 tablespoons lemon juice
5 tablespoons corn oil
8–10 large fresh green chillies,
   slit lengthways
8–10 curry leaves
½ teaspoon onion seeds
¼ teaspoon mustard seeds
3 onions, finely sliced
2 tablespoons chopped fresh
   coriander
3 hard-boiled eggs, halved,
to garnish

green chilli curry

(Mirch Ka Salan)

1 Put the tamarind into a bowl with 450 ml (¾ pint) of the hot water, mash with a fork and leave to soak for 1 hour.
2 Grind the sesame seeds in a spice grinder until very fine. Add the coconut, grind for 30–40 seconds. Remove and place in a bowl. Stir in the ground coriander, cumin, ginger, garlic, salt, turmeric and lemon juice. Set aside.
3 Heat the corn oil in a saucepan and fry the chillies for about 1 minute. Using a slotted spoon, remove the chillies and set aside, leaving behind as much oil as possible. In the same oil, fry the curry leaves, onion seeds, mustard seeds and sliced onions until golden brown.
4 Add the spice mixture and fry for 1–2 minutes, then pour in the remaining 150 ml (¼ pint) water, cover the pan with a lid and cook for 5–7 minutes.
5 While the spices are cooking, pour the tamarind into a sieve with a bowl set under it and squeeze out as much pulp as possible. Add a little more hot water to squeeze out any more pulp. Turn the pulp into the saucepan and stir it in well, then add the fried green chillies and fresh coriander. Cook for 5 minutes, then stir-fry for 2 minutes before serving garnished with the hard-boiled eggs.

ingredients
**3 tablespoons good quality
extra virgin olive oil
½ teaspoon white cumin
seeds
1 green pepper, cored,
deseeded and thickly sliced
1 red pepper, cored, deseeded
and thickly sliced
1 orange pepper, cored,
deseeded and thickly sliced
2 courgettes, diagonally sliced
2 tomatoes, halved
2 red onions, quartered
1 aubergine, thickly sliced
2 thick fresh green chillies,
sliced
4 garlic cloves
1 x 2.5 cm (1 inch) piece fresh
root ginger, shredded
1 teaspoon dried crushed
red chillies
1 tablespoon chopped fresh
coriander
½ teaspoon salt
lemon slices, to serve**

*These lightly spiced roast vegetables are delicious as a starter or a side
dish. Although I have called them roast vegetables, I actually prefer to
cook them in a large heavy-based grill pan. I have suggested a selection
of vegetables, but you may use whatever varieties you prefer.*

spicy roast vegetables

1 Heat the grill pan for 2 minutes. Pour in the olive oil, then add the cumin
seeds. Lower the heat to medium.
2 Arrange the vegetables in the pan with a pair of tongs, then add the green
chillies, garlic, ginger, red chillies, fresh coriander and salt and increase the
heat. Cook the vegetables for 7–10 minutes, turning them with the tongs.
3 Serve hot with lemon slices.

*It is important to use freshly diced garlic cloves for this dish as it gives the
whole dish a beautiful aroma. Although I have suggested French beans
and baby corn, you can use any vegetables of your choice.*

balti stir-fried french beans and baby corn in garlic butter

ingredients
**2 tablespoons chopped fresh
coriander
1 teaspoon chopped fresh mint
1 teaspoon salt
1 teaspoon brown sugar
1 teaspoon lemon juice
75 g (3 oz) unsalted butter
1 tablespoon corn oil
6 garlic cloves, diced
1 teaspoon onion seeds
1 teaspoon crushed dried
red chillies
12–14 baby onions
300 g (10 oz) French beans
300 g (10 oz) baby corn
1 teaspoon freshly ground
pepper**

1 In a small bowl, mix together the fresh coriander, mint, salt, brown sugar
and lemon juice.
2 Heat the butter with the oil in a balti pan, karahi or wok and fry the garlic,
onion seeds and red chillies for about 1 minute.
3 Add the fresh coriander and mint mixture, baby onions, French beans and
baby corn and stir-fry for 5–7 minutes over a medium heat.
4 Finally, sprinkle with the pepper and serve immediately.

ingredients

4 tablespoons corn oil
2 onions, sliced
1 teaspoon ginger pulp
1 teaspoon garlic pulp
1 teaspoon ground coriander
1 teaspoon chilli powder
¼ teaspoon turmeric
1 teaspoon salt
1 x 425 g (14 oz) can tomatoes
2 tablespoons chopped fresh coriander
2 whole fresh green chillies, halved
3 hard-boiled eggs, halved, to serve

This stir-fry is quickly prepared and is ideal as an accompaniment to almost any meat dish. Garnish with halved hard-boiled eggs and serve with Plain Boiled Rice (see page 93).

quick stir-fried
tomatoes and onions

1 Heat the oil in a saucepan, add the onions and fry until soft. Lower the heat, add the ginger, garlic, ground coriander, chilli powder, turmeric and salt and stir for about 1 minute. Pour in the canned tomatoes with their juices and cook over a high heat for about 5 minutes.
2 Add the fresh coriander and green chillies and cook for 1 minute. Serve with the hard-boiled eggs.

ingredients

2 onions, sliced
6–8 curry leaves
¼ teaspoon mustard seeds
1 teaspoon shredded fresh root ginger
3 garlic cloves, roughly sliced
4 tablespoons corn oil
300 g (10 oz) mushrooms, halved
175 g (6 oz) mangetout
175 g (6 oz) baby corn
3 fresh red chillies, sliced
2 tablespoons sesame seeds
1 tablespoon chopped fresh coriander
1 teaspoon salt
½ teaspoon sugar

Though mangetout is not really an Indian vegetable, I like to use it as it has a nice crunchy texture. This tasty dish makes an excellent accompaniment to almost anything.

haandi mushroom
and mangetout stir-fry

1 Place the onions in a haandi or a deep frying pan with the curry leaves, mustard seeds, shredded ginger and garlic cloves. Pour in the oil and fry over a high heat, stirring occasionally, for about 3 minutes.
2 Add the mushrooms, mangetout and baby corn and fry for 2–3 minutes, then stir in the red chillies, sesame seeds and fresh coriander. Finally, sprinkle with the salt and sugar and stir them in.
3 Serve immediately.

A delicious stew made with vegetables and red kidney beans, this dish is particularly suitable for vegetarians as the red kidney beans are a good source of protein.

vegetable stew

1 Heat the oil in a saucepan and stir-fry the sweet potatoes, potatoes, carrots and French beans for 3–5 minutes. Remove the vegetables from the pan with a slotted spoon and set aside. Try to leave as much oil as possible in the pan.

2 Fry the onions until soft, then lower the heat. Add the garlic, cumin, ground coriander, chilli powder, salt, sugar, vinegar and red kidney beans and stir-fry for about 1 minute. Add the fried sweet potatoes, potatoes, carrots and French beans, pour in the water, cover and simmer for 5–7 minutes. Check to see that all the vegetables are tender and cooked, but not mushy.

3 Finally, add the cherry tomatoes to the pan and cook for 2 minutes more, then serve the stew at once.

ingredients

4 tablespoons corn oil
500 g (1 lb) sweet potatoes, peeled and cut into large dice
250 g (8 oz) potatoes, peeled and cut into large dice
2 carrots, sliced
250 g (8 oz) French beans, defrosted if frozen
2 onions, sliced
1½ teaspoons garlic pulp
1 teaspoon ground cumin
1 teaspoon ground coriander
1 teaspoon chilli powder
1 teaspoon salt
1 teaspoon sugar
3 tablespoons vinegar
75 g (3 oz) red kidney beans, cooked or canned
300 ml (½ pint) water
6–8 cherry tomatoes

ingredients

2 carrots, cut into thin strips
2 potatoes, cut into thin strips
125 g (4 oz) thin French beans
75 g (3 oz) frozen peas,
  defrosted
1 large red pepper, cored,
  deseeded and cut into strips
4 tablespoons corn oil
2 onions, sliced
¼ teaspoon mustard seeds
4–6 curry leaves
3 fresh green chillies, chopped
1 teaspoon poppy seeds
1 teaspoon desiccated coconut
175 ml (6 fl oz) coconut milk
1 teaspoon salt
1 tablespoon lemon juice
1 tablespoon chopped fresh
  coriander
150 ml (¼ pint) water

Highly spiced and very flavoursome, this delicious mixed vegetable stir-fry is always popular. It is very versatile and can be served as an accompaniment to almost anything.

balti mixed vegetables
in coconut sauce

1 Put the prepared carrots, potatoes, French beans, peas and red pepper into a bowl of water until you are ready to cook them.

2 Heat the oil in a balti pan, karahi or deep frying pan, add the onions, mustard seeds and curry leaves and fry for about 3 minutes.

3 Drain the water from the vegetables, add the vegetables to the balti pan and stir gently to mix. Stir in the green chillies, poppy seeds, desiccated coconut, coconut milk, salt, lemon juice, half of the fresh coriander and the measured water, cover the pan and cook over a low heat for 5–7 minutes. Garnish with the remaining coriander and serve at once.

haandi potatoes with
lime and coriander

ingredients

4 whole garlic cloves
1 teaspoon crushed coriander
  seeds
½ teaspoon crushed black
  peppercorns
1 tablespoon shredded root
  ginger
4 tablespoons corn oil
2 large bunches spring onions,
  finely chopped
15 baby potatoes, cut into
  5 mm (¼ inch) slices
1 large bunch fresh coriander,
  finely chopped, including the
  stalks
300 ml (½ pint) water
1 tablespoon sesame seeds
juice of 1 lime
1–2 fresh green chillies, finely
  chopped

1 Mix together the garlic cloves, crushed coriander seeds, crushed black peppercorns and half of the shredded ginger.

2 Heat the oil in a haandi or saucepan, add the spring onions and fry for about 1 minute.

3 Pour in the spice mixture, lower the heat and add the potatoes and half of the fresh coriander and stir-fry for 2 minutes, using a wooden spoon.

4 Pour in the water, cover the haandi and simmer for about 10 minutes or until the potatoes are cooked.

5 Add the remaining fresh coriander and ginger, the sesame seeds, lime juice and green chillies and cook for 2 minutes. Serve hot with chapati.

opposite: balti mixed vegetables in coconut sauce

I love using new potatoes, not only are they attractive to look at, but they are also very easy to cook and taste delicious. Cook the potatoes first as this helps them retain their shape and texture.

baby potatoes with whole spices and peppers

(Aloo Aur Simla Mirch)

1 Cook the potatoes in salted boiling water for 10–12 minutes until they are just tender. Check with a skewer to make sure they are cooked through.
2 Heat the oil in a large frying pan, add the mixed seeds and fry for about 30 seconds. Lower the heat, add the garlic, ginger, dried red chillies, curry leaves, onions and salt and cook for 1½–2 minutes.
3 Add the courgette and sliced peppers and cook for 5–7 minutes.
4 Turn the heat to high and stir-fry all the vegetables for 2–3 minutes. Add the cooked potatoes and stir gently so they absorb some of the spicy flavour. Sprinkle with the sesame seeds, cover the frying pan with a lid and cook for 2 minutes before serving.

ingredients
12–14 baby potatoes, halved
4 tablespoons corn oil
**1 heaped teaspoon mixed
   onion seeds, mustard seeds,
   white cumin seeds and
   crushed coriander seeds**
3 whole garlic cloves
**1 teaspoon shredded fresh
   root ginger**
6 dried red chillies
10–12 curry leaves
2 onions, sliced
1 teaspoon salt
1 large courgette, thickly sliced
**1 green pepper, cored,
   deseeded and roughly sliced**
**1 red pepper, cored, deseeded
   and roughly sliced**
**1 yellow pepper, cored,
   deseeded and roughly sliced**
2 tablespoons sesame seeds

Aloo methi (potatoes with fenugreek) is a traditional combination, which probably originated in Hyderabad. Use only a few fenugreek leaves as they can become bitter. Fenugreek leaves freeze very well and when used straight from frozen are almost as good as fresh ones.

ingredients
4 tablespoons corn oil
2 onions, diced
4–6 curry leaves
½ teaspoon onion seeds
½ teaspoon mustard seeds
½ teaspoon white cumin seeds
4 dried red chillies
1 teaspoon ginger pulp
1 teaspoon garlic pulp
1 large pinch turmeric
1 teaspoon chilli powder
1 teaspoon salt
3 potatoes, peeled and diced
1 tablespoon lemon juice
**2 tablespoons chopped
   fenugreek**
1 tomato, diced, to garnish

potatoes with fresh fenugreek

(Haandi Aloo Methi)

1 Heat the oil in a medium-sized haandi or saucepan and stir-fry the onions for 1 minute with the curry leaves, onion seeds, mustard seeds, cumin seeds and dried red chillies. Lower the heat and add the ginger, garlic, turmeric, chilli powder and salt and stir-fry for 2–3 minutes.
2 Add the potatoes, lemon juice and fenugreek, lower the heat further, cover the pan with a lid and cook for 7–10 minutes until the potatoes are tender.
3 Transfer to a serving dish and serve garnished with the diced tomato.

In this recipe cooked baby potatoes and okra are fried together and then added to a spicy sauce which is made with onions and spices and flavoured with tamarind pulp. It is delicious served as a side dish at a dinner party.

spicy **potatoes and okra**

(Masala Aloo Bhindi)

ingredients
- **1 tablespoon tomato purée**
- **2 tablespoons tamarind paste**
- **450 ml (¾ pint) water**
- **8 tablespoons corn oil**
- **½ teaspoon mixed onion seeds and mustard seeds**
- **6–8 curry leaves**
- **4 onions, sliced**
- **250 ml (8 fl oz) coconut milk**
- **50 g (2 oz) ground sesame seeds**
- **1 teaspoon ground cumin**
- **2 teaspoons ground coriander**
- **1 teaspoon ginger pulp**
- **1 teaspoon salt**
- **¼ teaspoon turmeric**
- **1 teaspoon garlic pulp**
- **1 teaspoon chilli powder**
- **corn oil, for frying**
- **250 g (8 oz) okra, trimmed**
- **8–10 baby potatoes, halved and boiled**
- **2 tablespoons chopped fresh coriander**
- **2 fresh red chillies, roughly chopped**

1 Mix the tomato purée, tamarind paste and 150 ml (¼ pint) of the measured water in a small bowl and set aside.

2 Heat 5 tablespoons of the oil in a haandi or a heavy-based saucepan, add the onion seeds, mustard seeds and the curry leaves and fry for about 30 seconds, then add the onions and fry until golden brown.

3 Meanwhile, in a mixing bowl, blend together the coconut milk, ground sesame seeds, ground cumin, ground coriander, ginger pulp, salt, turmeric, garlic pulp and chilli powder. Pour the mixture on to the onions in the pan and stir-fry for 2–3 minutes. Pour in the remaining measured water, cover the pan and simmer for about 5 minutes, stirring occasionally. When the onions and spices are cooked and the sauce has thickened, remove the pan from the heat and set aside.

4 Heat the remaining 3 tablespoons of the corn oil in a karahi or deep frying pan, add the okra and cooked potatoes and fry for about 5 minutes. Remove the vegetables from the pan with a slotted spoon, draining as much oil as possible, and add them to the pan with the onion sauce.

5 Return the pan to the heat, add the chopped fresh coriander and chopped red chillies and gently heat through the vegetables. Transfer to a serving dish and serve at once.

Serve this curry with a dhaal and Chapati (see page 112); it makes an excellent vegetarian meal. Cauliflower bhujia also makes a good accompaniment to most meat and chicken dishes.

haandi cauliflower
bhujia with fried potatoes
(Haandi Aloo Gobi)

ingredients

4 tablespoons corn oil, plus
   extra for deep-frying
2 large potatoes, diced
¼ teaspoon onion seeds
6–8 curry leaves
¼ teaspoon mustard seeds
3 dried red chillies (optional)
3 whole garlic cloves
2 onions, diced
1 teaspoon ginger pulp
1 teaspoon chilli powder
1 teaspoon salt
1 cauliflower, cut into
   small florets
1 tablespoon lemon juice
2 tablespoons chopped fresh
   coriander
2 fresh green chillies
2 fresh red chillies
300 ml (½ pint) water

1 Heat the oil for deep-frying in a karahi or a deep frying pan, add the potatoes and deep-fry for 3–5 minutes. Remove from the pan with a slotted spoon and drain on kitchen paper.
2 Heat the 4 tablespoons oil in a haandi or heavy-based saucepan, add the onion seeds, curry leaves, mustard seeds, dried red chillies, garlic and onions and fry until the onions are soft golden brown.
3 Stir in the ginger, chilli powder and salt, then add half the cauliflower florets, the lemon juice, 1 tablespoon of the fresh coriander and the fresh green and red chillies.
4 Pour in the measured water, cover the haandi, lower the heat and leave to cook for 5–7 minutes.
5 Add the remaining cauliflower and stir-fry for a further 5–7 minutes, so you have some soft cauliflower and some crunchy florets.
6 Finally, stir in the fried potatoes and heat through. Serve hot, garnished with the remaining fresh coriander.

Pine kernels are not used a great deal in India today, but I like to use them as they add a crunchy texture to this dish. Good quality, ready peeled pine kernels are available from most supermarkets.

spinach with pine kernels

ingredients

1 kg (2 lb) fresh spinach
50 g (2 oz) unsalted butter
1 tablespoon corn oil
1 teaspoon garlic pulp
1 teaspoon ginger pulp
1 teaspoon chilli powder
¼ teaspoon turmeric
1 teaspoon salt
75 g (3 oz) pine kernels

1 Wash the spinach thoroughly, chop roughly and place in a saucepan with the water left on the leaves. Bring to the boil, then drain thoroughly in a sieve and set aside.
2 Heat the butter with the oil in a saucepan, then remove the saucepan from the heat and add the garlic, ginger, chilli powder, turmeric, salt and drained spinach and stir together.
3 Return the saucepan to the heat, add the pine kernels and cook gently for about 2 minutes. Serve hot with freshly made Chapati (see page 112).

opposite: haandi cauliflower bhujia with fried potatoes, plain boiled rice and naan bread

This vegetable dish has a final sprinkling of roasted sesame seeds which gives it a crunchy texture. Although roasted sesame seeds are available in delicatessens, they taste better if you dry roast them yourself in a frying pan to make them crunchier.

french beans with potatoes and roasted sesame seeds

ingredients
4 tablespoons oil
2 onions, diced
⅛ teaspoon onion seeds
6 curry leaves
3 potatoes, cut into 5 mm (¼ inch) slices
125 g (4 oz) French beans, cut into short lengths
about 150 ml (¼ pint) water
2 fresh red chillies, sliced

spice paste:
3 tablespoons sesame seeds
2 teaspoons ground coriander
1 teaspoon ground cumin
1 teaspoon ginger pulp
1 teaspoon garlic pulp
1 teaspoon chilli powder
1 teaspoon salt
1 tablespoon lemon juice

1 First make the spice paste. Reserve 1 tablespoon of the sesame seeds, place the remainder in a spice grinder and grind to a fine paste. Put the powdered sesame into a bowl and blend to a paste with the ground coriander, cumin, ginger, garlic, chilli powder, salt and lemon juice. Set aside.
2 Dry roast the reserved sesame seeds as above until they jump vigourously. Set aside.
3 Heat the oil in a haandi, add the onions, onion seeds and curry leaves and fry until the onions are soft golden brown.
4 Pour in the spice paste, lower the heat and fry for about 1 minute, stirring constantly. Add the potatoes and beans and stir-fry for 1–2 minutes.
5 Pour in the water, cover and cook for 5–7 minutes or until the potatoes are tender. Stir-fry for 1 minute, then stir in the red chillies. Serve garnished with the reserved roasted sesame seeds.

ingredients
4 tablespoons corn oil
4 curry leaves
2 onions, sliced
1½ teaspoons ground coriander
1 teaspoon ginger pulp
1 teaspoon garlic pulp
1 teaspoon chilli powder
1 teaspoon salt
300 g (10 oz) frozen sweetcorn
1 small red pepper, cored, deseeded and diced
2 spring onions, finely chopped

Simple to make, this curry makes a very good accompaniment. In fact, it is a good idea always to keep some sweetcorn in the freezer so you can make this dish quickly for unexpected guests.

spicy sweetcorn curry

1 Heat the oil in a saucepan, add the curry leaves and onions and fry until soft. Lower the heat slightly and add the ground coriander, ginger, garlic, chilli powder and salt and stir-fry for about 30 seconds. Add the sweetcorn and fry for about 5 minutes or until all the water has evaporated. Stir in the diced pepper and spring onions and serve at once.

opposite: french beans with potatoes and roasted sesame seeds, poppadums and mango milkshake (see page 125)

The okra is fried to a crisp golden brown and then added to the soft moong dhaal. The two contrasting textures make this dish very special. Serve with hot paratas or chapati.

balti moong dhaal
with fried okra

(Bhindi Aur Moong ki Dhaal)

1 Heat the oil in a balti pan, karahi or deep frying pan and fry the okra, in batches for 3–5 minutes, until crisp and golden. Lift out with a slotted spoon and drain on kitchen paper. Set aside the frying pan with the remaining oil.
2 Wash the moong dhaal thoroughly, then boil in unsalted water over a medium heat for 5–7 minutes until soft but not mushy. Drain and set aside.
3 Meanwhile, return the frying pan to the heat, add the onions and fry until golden brown. Stir in the ginger, garlic, ground coriander, chilli powder, salt and half of the fresh coriander. Add the tomatoes and moong dhaal and stir-fry for 3–5 minutes.
4 Finally, stir in the fried okra and the remaining fresh coriander.

ingredients
4 tablespoons corn oil
250 g (8 oz) okra, trimmed and cut into 1 cm (½ inch) slices
175 g (6 oz) moong dhaal
2 onions, sliced
1 teaspoon ginger pulp
1 teaspoon garlic pulp
1½ teaspoons ground coriander
1 teaspoon chilli powder
1½ teaspoons salt
2 tablespoons chopped fresh coriander
3 tomatoes, sliced

This delicious blend of chana dhaal and okra makes an unusual way of serving a vegetable with a good source of protein. Try to choose small okra for this dish.

haandi chana dhaal
with okra

1 Wash the chana dhaal, then boil for about 10 minutes until it is soft but not mushy. Check by rubbing the dhaal between your index finger and thumb.
2 Drain, cover and set aside.
3 Heat 4 tablespoons of the oil in a haandi or saucepan, add the diced onion, mustard seeds and curry leaves and fry until soft.
4 Add the garlic, ginger, chillies, salt and tomato purée, reduce the heat and stir-fry for 1 minute. Pour in the water, cover, and simmer for 3–5 minutes.
5 Heat the remaining oil in a frying pan, add the okra and fry for 3–5 minutes, stirring so they fry equally on all sides. Transfer the okra to the haandi, stir in the chana dhaal and stir-fry for 2 minutes.
6 Garnish with the fresh coriander and serve hot.

ingredients
2 tablespoons chana dhaal
7 tablespoons corn oil
1 onion, finely diced
¼ teaspoon mustard seeds
4 curry leaves
4 garlic cloves, sliced
1 x 3.5 cm (1½ inch) piece fresh root ginger, shredded
1½ teaspoons crushed dried chillies
1 teaspoon salt
1 tablespoon tomato purée
300 ml (½ pint) water
500 g (1 lb) okra, trimmed
1 tablespoon chopped fresh coriander, to garnish

ingredients

300 g (10 oz) panir, cubed
12–14 canned pineapple cubes,
juice reserved
1 large green pepper, cored,
deseeded and cut into large
dice
1 large red pepper, cored,
deseeded and cut into large
dice
10 baby onions
10 cherry tomatoes
2 courgettes, thickly sliced
½ teaspoon salt
1 teaspoon chilli powder
1 teaspoon ginger pulp
1 teaspoon ground coriander
1 tablespoon tomato purée
1 tablespoon chopped fresh
coriander
oil, for brushing
lettuce, to serve

Panir is a cheese eaten widely in India as it is a good source of protein, especially for the very strict vegetarian. This is a most unusual way of serving it, with a tasty sweet and sour flavour from the pineapple cubes. Serve as a starter or as part of a meal. Blocks of panir can be bought at most Indian and Pakistani grocers and some high street supermarkets.

panir tikka

1 Place the panir, pineapple cubes, diced green and red peppers, baby onions, cherry tomatoes and courgettes in a bowl and pour over a little of the pinepapple juice from the can.
2 In a separate bowl, mix together the salt, chilli powder, ginger, ground coriander, tomato purée and fresh coriander.
3 Arrange the panir, pineapple cubes and vegetables on skewers and place in a heatproot dish. Pour over the spice mixture. Brush with a little oil and cook in a preheated oven, 220°C (425°F), Gas Mark 7, for 5–7 minutes. Serve immediately on a bed of lettuce.

ingredients

5 tablespoons corn oil
250 g (8 oz) panir, cubed
3 onions, sliced
1 large pinch onion seeds
4–6 curry leaves
1 large pinch mustard seeds
1 teaspoon ginger pulp
1 teaspoon chilli powder
1 teaspoon ground cumin
1½ teaspoons ground coriander
1 teaspoon garlic pulp
¼ teaspoon turmeric
1 teaspoon salt
1 teaspoon tamarind paste
½ teaspoon sugar
1 x 425 g (14 oz) can
tomatoes, chopped
1 green pepper, cored,
deseeded and roughly diced
1 orange pepper, cored,
deseeded and roughly diced
1 tablespoon chopped fresh
coriander

The combination of tomatoes and panir is delicious served with freshly made hot chapatis. Use peppers of one colour, or a mixture of colours as this makes the dish look very attractive on the dinner table.

panir with tomatoes and peppers

1 Heat the oil in a large frying pan, add the panir cubes and fry for about 1 minute, turning them all the time. Remove from the pan with a slotted spoon and drain on kitchen paper.
2 In the same oil fry the onions with the onion seeds, curry leaves and the mustard seeds for 3 minutes.
3 Lower the heat, add the ginger, chilli powder, cumin, ground coriander, garlic, turmeric, salt, tamarind paste and sugar and stir-fry quickly for about 2 minutes.
4 Stir in the canned tomatoes and cook for 1 minute, then add the diced green und orange peppers, panir cubes and fresh coriander. Cover the pan, lower the heat and cook for about 3 minutes before serving.

rice, pulses and lentils

saffron rice moulds
with sweetcorn and peas

1 Wash the rice, drain and set aside in a sieve.
2 Heat the corn oil with the butter in a heavy-based saucepan and fry the green cardamoms, cloves and cinnamon for about 40 seconds. Add the drained rice, salt, saffron strands, sweetcorn and peas and stir-fry gently over a medium heat for about 1 minute. Pour in the water, cover with a lid and cook for 15–20 minutes.
3 Remove the pan from the heat and let the rice stand for 5 minutes.
4 Meanwhile, lightly grease 6 ramekins with butter. Divide the rice equally among the ramekins and press down with the back of a spoon. Set aside.
5 When you are ready to serve the rice, reheat the moulds, preferably in a microwave for 3–5 minutes. To serve, run a knife around the moulds and turn them upside down on to individual plates.
6 Serve as an accompaniment to any of the chicken, lamb or vegetable dishes.

ingredients
400 g (13 oz) Basmati rice
1 tablespoon corn oil
75 g (3 oz) butter, plus extra for greasing
4 green cardamoms
3 cloves
1 cinnamon stick
1 teaspoon salt
1 teaspoon saffron strands
50 g (2 oz) frozen sweetcorn
50 g (2 oz) frozen peas
750 ml (1¼ pints) water

chicken **biryani**

(Murgh Biryani)

1 Pour the milk into a measuring jug. Crush the saffron strands, add to the milk and set aside.
2 Wash the rice until the water runs clear, set aside in a bowl of water to soak.
3 To cook the chicken, heat the ghee in a medium haandi or heavy-based saucepan and fry the onions until golden brown. Set aside about 1 tablespoon of onions with some ghee and reserve. Add the black cardamoms, peppercorns, cloves, cinnamon stick, garam masala, ginger, garlic, chilli powder, turmeric and salt to the haandi and stir-fry over a low heat for about 45 seconds to mix and fry the spices.
4 Add the chicken and stir-fry for 5–7 minutes. Pour in the lemon juice and yogurt and add the fresh coriander and green chillies. Stir-fry for 5 minutes. Lower the heat, cover the haandi and cook for 7–10 minutes. Set aside.
5 To cook the rice, pour the measured water into a large haandi and add the cinnamon, black cardamoms, peppercorns, half the fresh coriander and salt and bring to the boil. Drain the rice thoroughly in a sieve, then tip it into the boiling water and part-cook for 5–7 minutes. When the water returns to the boil, check the rice by rubbing a few grains between your index finger and thumb. When you can feel a hard core in the centre with a soft exterior, then the rice is part-cooked.
6 Drain the rice and return half of it to the haandi. Place the chicken pieces on top, then add half of the saffron milk, half of the lemon juice, the remaining fresh coriander and half of the chopped green fresh chillies.
7 Arrange the remaining rice on top and add the remaining saffron milk, lemon juice and chopped green chillies, and the reserved fried onions in ghee. Cover the haandi with foil and then the lid and cook for 12–15 minutes. Finally, mix thoroughly and serve.

ingredients
175 ml (6 fl oz) milk
1 teaspoon saffron strands
400 g (13 oz) Basmati rice
900 ml (1½ pints) water
1 cinnamon stick
2 black cardamoms
4 peppercorns
2 tablespoons chopped fresh coriander
2 teaspoons salt
2 tablespoons lemon juice
4 fresh green chillies, chopped

for the chicken:
6 tablespoons vegetable ghee
2 onions, thinly sliced
3 black cardamoms
4 black peppercorns
2 whole cloves
1 cinnamon stick
2 teaspoons garam masala
2 teaspoons ginger pulp
1 teaspoon garlic pulp
1 teaspoon chilli powder
¼ teaspoon turmeric
1 teaspoon salt
1 x 1.5 kg (3 lb) chicken, skinned and cut into 8–10 pieces
2 tablespoons lemon juice
4 tablespoons natural yogurt
2 tablespoons chopped fresh coriander
2 fresh green chillies, slit in the middle

previous page from left: chicken biryani and saffron rice moulds with sweetcorn and peas

If you like cooking curries, it is always a good idea to have a packet of good quality Basmati rice in your larder. This recipe is probably one of the easiest in the world and, of course, extremely versatile. Rice should be washed thoroughly in warm water, rubbing it with your fingers. Wash it at least three times and drain in a sieve.

plain **boiled rice**

ingredients
400 g (13 oz) Basmati rice
750 ml (1¼ pints) water
1 teaspoon salt
knob of butter (optional)

1 Wash the rice thoroughly and drain in a sieve. Place it in a heavy-based saucepan, pour in the water, add the salt and bring to the boil over a high heat. Reduce the heat to medium low, add the butter, if using, cover with a tightly fitting lid and cook for 12–15 minutes. When the rice is cooked, leave it to stand, covered, for 5 minutes before serving.

quick and easy **bay fried rice**

ingredients
400 g (13 oz) Basmati rice
3 tablespoons vegetable ghee
1 onion, sliced
2 fresh bay leaves
2 cloves
2 black cardamoms
4 black peppercorns
1 teaspoon salt
1½ teaspoons ginger pulp
1½ teaspoons garlic pulp
750 ml (1¼ pints) water

1 Wash the rice thoroughly and leave it to soak in a bowl.
2 Heat the ghee in a heavy-based saucepan, add the onion and fry until golden brown. Add the bay leaves, cloves, cardamoms and black peppercorns and stir-fry for 2–3 minutes, then add the salt, ginger and garlic. Drain the rice, then add it to the pan and stir-fry for 1 minute.
3 Pour in the water and bring to the boil. Reduce the heat to medium, cover the pan and cook for 15–20 minutes or until all the water has been absorbed and the rice is cooked. Leave to stand for 5 minutes before serving.

haandi boiled rice
with buttered saffron

(Khushka Aur Makhan May Zafraan)

ingredients
400 g (13 oz) Basmati rice
½ teaspoon salt
750 ml (1¼ pints) water
75 g (3 oz) unsalted butter
1 tablespoon corn oil
¼ teaspoon cardamom seeds
1 teaspoon crushed saffron strands

1 Wash the rice until the water runs clear, then drain through a sieve.
2 Place the rice in a haandi or saucepan with the salt and water and bring to the boil.
3 Reduce the heat to medium, cover the pan and cook for 12–15 minutes or until the rice is cooked and the water has been fully absorbed. Set aside.
4 Heat the butter with the oil in a small frying pan. Throw in the cardamom seeds and saffron and immediately remove the pan from the heat. Pour the spice mixture quickly over the cooked rice. Leave to stand for 5–7 minutes before serving.

haandi rice with cumin

(Haandi Chawal with Zeera)

ingredients
400 g (13 oz) Basmati rice
3 tablespoons corn oil
1 teaspoon white cumin seeds
6 curry leaves
4–6 dried red chillies (optional)
1 teaspoon salt
750 ml (1¼ pints) water
1 tablespoon chopped fresh coriander

1 Wash the rice well, drain and set aside.
2 Heat the oil in a haandi and fry the cumin seeds, curry leaves and dried red chillies, if using, for about 1 minute. Add the rice and stir gently with a slotted spoon for about 1 minute.
3 Add the salt, water and fresh coriander and bring to the boil. Lower the heat to medium, cover and cook for about 20 minutes. Check to see that the rice is cooked and the water has been fully absorbed.
4 Remove the haandi from the heat and leave it to stand for 5–7 minutes before serving the rice.

A very versatile and delicious rice which is lightly spiced and fried and goes together well with the peas and fried potatoes. Always use a good quality Basmati rice for this dish.

rice with fried potatoes and peas

ingredients
400 g (13 oz) Basmati rice
2 tablespoons vegetable ghee
2 black cardamoms
4 black peppercorns
¼ teaspoon black cumin seeds
2 onions, sliced
1 teaspoon ginger pulp
1 teaspoon garlic pulp
1 teaspoon salt
2 fresh green chillies, sliced
2 tablespoons chopped fresh coriander
75 g (3 oz) peas, fresh or frozen
750 ml (1¼ pints) water
approximately 300 ml (½ pint) oil, for deep-frying
3 potatoes, diced

1 Wash the rice until the water runs clear and set aside in a bowl of water to soak.
2 Heat the ghee in a heavy-based saucepan and fry the cardamoms, peppercorns and black cumin seeds for about 30–40 seconds, then add the onions and fry until soft golden brown.
3 Add the ginger, garlic, salt, green chillies and fresh coriander.
4 Drain the rice thoroughly, then add it to the onion and spices and stir-fry for 1 minute using a slotted spoon, making gentle movements so you do not damage the rice. Add the peas and water and bring to the boil. Lower the heat, cover the pan and cook for 15–20 minutes.
5 Meanwhile, heat the oil in a deep frying pan and fry the diced potatoes for 5–7 minutes over a medium heat until light golden brown. Remove with a slotted spoon and drain on kitchen paper.
6 When the rice is cooked, mix gently with the fried potatoes and serve.

This pulao rice has a delicious sweet and sour flavour. It makes a pleasant change from plain boiled or fried rice and goes well with most of the dishes in this book.

haandi **carrot pulao**

(Haandi Gajar Pulao)

1 Wash the rice until the water runs clear and leave in a bowl to soak.
2 Heat the butter with the corn oil in a large saucepan and fry the cardamoms, cinnamon and black cumin seeds over a medium heat for 1 minute. Lower the heat, add the onion and fry slowly for 3–5 minutes.
3 Meanwhile, whisk the yogurt in a bowl and add the salt, ginger, garlic, chilli powder, ground almonds, ground coconut, lemon juice, sugar and carrots.
4 Add the spice mixture to the onion and stir-fry for 3–5 minutes or until the mixture has thickened, forming a thick sauce.
5 Drain the rice thoroughly in a sieve, then add to the pan with the sultanas and flaked almonds. Blend everything together, then pour in the water and bring to the boil. Lower the heat, cover and cook for 15–20 minutes or until all the water has been absorbed.
6 Let the rice stand for 10 minutes, then transfer to a shallow dish and garnish with the grated carrot and fresh coriander.

ingredients
600 g (1 lb 2 oz) Basmati rice
125 g (4 oz) butter
1 tablespoon corn oil
3 green cardamoms
1 cinnamon stick
¼ teaspoon black cumin seeds
1 large onion, diced
150 ml (¼ pint) natural yogurt
1½ teaspoons salt
1 teaspoon ginger pulp
1 teaspoon garlic pulp
1 teaspoon chilli powder
1 tablespoon ground almonds
1 tablespoon ground coconut
1 tablespoon lemon juice
1 teaspoon sugar
2 carrots, sliced
50 g (2 oz) sultanas
25 g (1 oz) flaked almonds
1 litre (1¾ pints) water

to garnish:
1 carrot, grated
1 tablespoon chopped fresh coriander

Fenugreek leaves have a faintly bitter taste so are best mixed with something. Tomatoes and fenugreek go very well together and this recipe makes a delicious accompaniment to a good chicken curry.

rice with tomatoes and fenugreek

(Tamatar Methi Chawal)

1 Wash the rice until the water runs clear, set aside in a bowl of water to soak.
2 Heat the corn oil in a large heavy-based saucepan with the curry leaves, onion seeds, red chillies and onions and stir-fry for about 5 minutes. Add the ginger, garlic, tomatoes, fresh coriander, green chillies and salt and stir-fry over a medium heat for 2 minutes.
3 Drain the rice through a sieve, then tip it into the onion and tomato mixture. Pour in the measured water and bring to the boil over a high heat.
4 Lower the heat to medium, cover with a lid and cook for 15–20 minutes until the water has been absorbed and the rice is cooked. Let the rice stand for 5 minutes before serving.

ingredients
600 g (1 lb 2 oz) Basmati rice
4 tablespoons corn oil
4–6 curry leaves
½ teaspoon onion seeds
4 dried red chillies
2 onions, sliced
1 teaspoon ginger pulp
1 teaspoon garlic pulp
3 tomatoes, sliced
2 tablespoons chopped fresh coriander
2 fresh green chillies, chopped
1½ teaspoons salt
1 litre (1¾ pints) water

This rice dish goes particularly well with all the prawn dishes in this book. Fresh coconut always adds that extra flavour, but you can use desiccated coconut if you cannot find fresh.

lemon rice with coconut

ingredients
400 g (13 oz) Basmati rice
2 tablespoons corn oil
50 g (2 oz) butter
¼ teaspoon mustard seeds
12–15 curry leaves
¼ teaspoon turmeric
1 teaspoon salt
2 tablespoons lemon juice
2 tablespoons grated fresh coconut
750 ml (1¼ pints) water
1 tablespoon chopped fresh coriander, to garnish

1 Wash the Basmati rice until the water runs clear.
2 In a large saucepan, heat the oil with the butter until hot, then add the mustard seeds, curry leaves, turmeric and salt. Lower the heat (if the heat is still quite fierce, remove the pan from the heat), add the rice and return the pan to the heat, if removed. Stir the rice in well, using a wooden spoon.
3 Pour in the lemon juice, grated coconut and water and bring to the boil. Cover the pan and cook over a medium heat for 15–20 minutes until all the water has been absorbed and the rice is cooked.
4 Leave the rice to stand for 5–7 minutes before serving garnished with the chopped fresh coriander.

One of my favourite dishes, this is very easy to make and also makes a good dinner party dish. Always use a good quality Basmati rice; soaking it first prevents it from sticking during cooking.

king prawn and mushroom pulao

ingredients
400 g (13 oz) Basmati rice
1 tablespoon corn oil
125 g (4 oz) unsalted butter
½ teaspoon mixed mustard seeds and onion seeds
2 onions, sliced
6–8 curry leaves
1 teaspoon ginger pulp
1 teaspoon garlic pulp
¼ teaspoon turmeric
1 teaspoon chilli powder
1½ teaspoons ground coriander
1 heaped teaspoon tomato purée
1 teaspoon salt
2 tablespoons chopped fresh coriander
4–6 fresh red chillies, slit in the middle
500 g (1 lb) frozen cooked king prawns, defrosted and peeled
250 g (8 oz) mushrooms, halved
2 tablespoons lemon juice
150 ml (¼ pint) single cream
750 ml (1¼ pints) water

to garnish (optional):
hard-boiled eggs, halved
tomatoes, sliced

1 Wash the rice until the water runs clear, then leave in a bowl to soak.
2 Heat the oil with the butter in a large saucepan over a medium heat. Add the mustard and onion seeds and fry for about 1 minute, then add the onions and curry leaves and fry for about 3 minutes.
3 Meanwhile, mix together the ginger, garlic, turmeric, chilli powder, ground coriander, tomato purée and salt and pour the mixture on to the onions.
4 Fry the spice mixture for about 2 minutes, then add half of the fresh coriander, the red chillies, king prawns and mushrooms. Cook, stirring, over a medium high heat for about 5 minutes.
5 Drain the rice. Pour the lemon juice and cream into the saucepan, add the rice and cook for 3–5 minutes, stirring constantly.
6 Finally, pour in the water, add the remaining fresh coriander and bring to the boil. Lower the heat, cover the pan and cook for 15–20 minutes, or until the water has been fully absorbed and the rice is cooked.
7 Serve garnished with halved hard-boiled eggs and sliced tomatoes, if liked.

opposite: king prawn and mushroom pulao

haandi **chicken pulao**

ingredients

250 ml (8 fl oz) natural yogurt
1½ teaspoons ginger pulp
1½ teaspoons garlic pulp
1½ teaspoons salt
3 tablespoons lemon juice
1 x 750 g (1½ lb) whole chicken, cut into 8–10 pieces
4–5 tablespoons vegetable ghee
3 onions, sliced
1.5 litres (2½ pints) water
2 cinnamon sticks
3 black cardamoms
4 whole cloves
6 black peppercorns
2 tablespoons chopped fresh coriander
1½ teaspoons salt
600 g (1 lb 2 oz) Basmati rice
1 tablespoon kewra water, (see page 13)
1 teaspoon saffron strands, crushed

1 Pour the natural yogurt into a large mixing bowl. Add the ginger, garlic, salt and 2 tablespoons of the lemon juice and beat together. Add the chicken pieces and coat thoroughly with the spice mixture. Cover the bowl and leave to marinate for about 3 hours.
2 Heat the ghee in a haandi or heavy-based saucepan, add the onions and fry until golden brown. Remove about one-quarter of the onions and ghee from the pan and reserve.
3 Pour the chicken and yogurt mixture on to the remaining onions in the pan and cook, stirring, for 2–3 minutes. Reduce the heat to medium low, cover and cook for 12–15 minutes, stirring occasionally. When the chicken is ready, remove from the heat and set aside.
4 Pour the water into a large saucepan and bring to the boil with the cinnamon sticks, black cardamoms, cloves, peppercorns, fresh coriander and salt. Wash the rice, drain and add to the pan when the water begins to boil and part-cook for about 5–7 minutes. To check whether the rice is part-cooked, press a few grains between your finger and thumb; they should be soft on top and hard in the middle. Drain the rice through a sieve.
5 Return half of the rice to the saucepan. Place the chicken pieces on top and cover with the remaining rice. Add the reserved fried onions in ghee, the kewra water, crushed saffron strands and the remaining lemon juice. Cover the pan with a tight-fitting lid and cook for about 15–20 minutes over a low heat.
6 Check to see that the rice is fully cooked, then let it stand for 5–7 minutes. Mix thoroughly before serving.

biryani with marinated lamb and spices

ingredients

½ small papaya, peeled and roughly diced
750 g (1½ lb) leg of spring lamb, on the bone
1½ teaspoons ginger pulp
1½ teaspoons garlic pulp
1 teaspoon chilli powder
2½ teaspoons salt
1½ teaspoons garam masala
½ teaspoon ground cardamom
250 ml (8 fl oz) natural yogurt
600 g (1 lb 2 oz) Basmati rice
1 litre (1¾ pints) water
2 black cardamoms
1 cinnamon stick
¼ teaspoon black cumin seeds
2 tablespoons chopped fresh coriander
5 fresh green chillies
2 teaspoons saffron strands
125 ml (4 fl oz) warm milk
6 tablespoons ghee
4 onions, sliced
4 tablespoons lemon juice

1 Place the papaya in a food processor and work to a pulp. Rub half of the pulp over the lamb, cover and leave to tenderize for about 30 minutes.
2 Meanwhile, mix together the ginger, garlic, chilli powder, garam masala, 1½ teaspoons of the salt, ground cardamom and yogurt. Rub the spice mixture over the lamb, cover and set aside for 1 hour.
3 Wash the rice thoroughly and set aside. Bring the water to the boil in a large saucepan with the black cardamoms, cinnamon, black cumin seeds, the remaining 1 teaspoon salt, 1 tablespoon of the fresh coriander and 2 of the green chillies, sliced.
4 Once the water boils, add the rice and part-cook for 5–7 minutes. To check the rice is part-cooked, rub a grain between your thumb and index finger; when the top feels soft and the centre feels hard the rice is ready. Drain the rice through a sieve and set aside.
5 Crush the saffron strands in the milk and set aside.
6 Heat the ghee in a large heavy-based saucepan and fry the onions until soft golden brown. Remove about 1 tablespoon of the onions and 2 tablespoons of ghee and reserve. Lower the heat and place the lamb and rice on top of the onions. Top with the remaining fresh coriander, lemon juice, the 3 remaining green chillies, halved, the saffron and milk mixture and the reserved onions in ghee. Cover the pan with foil and then the lid and cook over a low heat for about 45 minutes. Check to see if the meat is cooked right through, then stir to mix and serve.

opposite: biryani with marinated lamb and spices

accompaniments, breads and snacks

A good accompaniment such as this raita can turn an ordinary meal into a memorable one. This is a delicious and unusual raita which is ideal with spicy dishes and can also be served as a dip.

raita with mango

(Kaim Ka Raita)

1 Place the mango, fresh coriander, green chillies, mint sauce, salt and sugar in a food processor and blend for about 2 minutes. Add the ground coriander and yogurt and blend for 30 seconds. Transfer the mixture into a bowl and stir in the diced cucumber.
2 Transfer the raita to a serving dish and garnish with a sprig of mint.

ingredients
1 unripe mango, peeled, stoned and roughly diced
2 tablespoons chopped fresh coriander
2 fresh green chillies
¼ teaspoon ready-made bottled mint sauce
1½ teaspoons salt
2 teaspoons sugar
1 teaspoon ground coriander
300 ml (½ pint) natural yogurt
½ cucumber, peeled and diced
sprig of mint, to garnish

Although there are a vast variety of ready-made chutneys on the market these days, I feel that making your own chutney with fresh ingredients is not only very satisfying, but also a tasty way of perking up a meal.

hot plum and apricot chutney

1 Place the apricots and plums in a saucepan. Pour in the vinegar, garam masala, chilli powder, ground coriander, cinnamon, salt and sugar and stir to mix. Bring it to the boil over a very low heat and then simmer gently for 15–20 minutes, then mash the fruit.
2 Remove the pan from the heat and set aside to cool. Once it has cooled, transfer the chutney into clean dry jars, cover and refrigerate. This chutney can be kept for about 2 weeks.

ingredients
5 fresh apricots, stoned and quartered
5 fresh plums, stoned and quartered
300 ml (½ pint) malt vinegar
1 teaspoon garam masala
½ teaspoon chilli powder
1½ teaspoons ground coriander
⅛ teaspoon ground cinnamon
1 teaspoon salt
4–6 tablespoons sugar

previous page, clockwise from top left: gram flour roti, raita with mango, and hot plum and apricot chutney

This is a very tasty roti which is fairly easy to make. It is often served with Baigun Ka Bhurta (see page 114). The recipe makes 6–8 roti.

gram flour roti
(Besani roti)

ingredients
175 g (6 oz) ata (chapati flour)
75 g (3 oz) gram flour
1 small onion, finely chopped
1 fresh green chilli, finely chopped
1 tablespoon chopped fresh coriander
1 teaspoon salt
1 teaspoon crushed dried red chillies
approximately 150 ml (¼ pint) water, to make a soft dough
2–3 tablespoons corn oil
flour, for dusting

1 Sift the ata and gram flour into a mixing bowl. Mix together the chopped onion and green chilli, fresh coriander, salt and crushed red chillies, then add them to the flour.
2 Stir in enough cold water to make a soft dough. Cover and set aside for about 30 minutes.
3 Divide the dough into 6–8 portions and shape it into flat rounds. Roll out each dough round on a lightly floured surface to 12–15 cm (5–6 inches) in diameter.
4 Heat a thawa or non-stick frying pan. Pick up each roti and gently place on the thawa. Grease the top with about 1 teaspoon oil and cook for about 30 seconds, turning over the roti twice with a spatula and pressing it down so that it cooks equally all over. Serve hot.

A delicious sweet and sour chutney which combines the distinctive flavours of dates and tamarind. This chutney can be served with almost anything.

date and tamarind chutney
(Khajoor Aur Imli Ki Chutney)

ingredients
250 g (8 oz) dried stoned dates, chopped
2 teaspoons tamarind paste
1 teaspoon tomato purée
4 tablespoons sugar
1 teaspoon ground ginger
1½ teaspoons ground coriander
1½ teaspoons chilli powder
1 teaspoon salt
125 ml (4 fl oz) malt vinegar
250 ml (8 fl oz) water

1 Place the dates, tamarind paste, tomato purée, sugar, ginger, ground coriander, chilli powder, salt, vinegar and water in a saucepan and bring to the boil over a medium high heat. Reduce the heat to low and cook for 7–10 minutes. Remove from the heat and set aside to cool.
2 Place all the mixture in a food processor and grind for about 1 minute or until the sauce looks very smooth. Transfer to a clean dry jar, cover and refrigerate. This chutney will keep for about 2 weeks.

ingredients

250 g (8 oz) brown sugar
1 teaspoon salt
1 teaspoon garam masala
1 teaspoon chilli powder
1 cinnamon stick
300 ml (½ pint) water
4 large unripe green mangoes, peeled, stoned and roughly sliced

One of the most popular chutneys, especially in the west where people eat it with poppadums as an appetizer before a meal. This is a very simple version, and quick to make.

simple sweet and sour
mango chutney

1 Place the brown sugar, salt, garam masala, chilli powder, cinnamon and measured water in a saucepan. Stir to mix and bring gently to the boil.
2 Drop in the mango slices, lower the heat and cook, covered, for 5–7 minutes until the mangoes have softened. Remove the saucepan lid and cook for a further 5 minutes or until the syrup has thickened.
3 Spoon the chutney into a bowl to cool. When cooled, transfer to a clean dry jar, cover and refrigerate. This will keep for 1–2 days in the refrigerator.

ingredients

8 tomatoes, diced
1½ teaspoons ground coriander
1 teaspoon ground cumin
1 teaspoon fresh ginger pulp
1 teaspoon fresh garlic pulp
1 teaspoon chilli powder
⅛ teaspoon turmeric
1 teaspoon salt
3 tablespoons corn oil
4–6 curry leaves
¼ teaspoon white cumin seeds
¼ teaspoon onion seeds
3 whole dried red chillies (optional)
1 onion, sliced
2 tablespoons lemon juice
1 tablespoon chopped fresh coriander

This chunky, spicy chutney is a simple but delicious accompaniment which can be made equally well with either fresh or canned tomatoes and which always proves popular.

tomato **chutney**

1 Place the tomatoes in a bowl with the ground coriander, cumin, ginger, garlic, chilli powder, turmeric and salt. Set aside.
2 Heat the oil in a saucepan, add the curry leaves, white cumin seeds, onion seeds, red chillies, if using, and onion and fry for about 1 minute. Add the tomato and spice mixture and stir-fry over a medium heat for 3–5 minutes.
3 Pour in the lemon juice and chopped fresh coriander and stir-fry for a further 5 minutes. Transfer to a dish and serve. This chutney can be kept in the refrigerator for 2 days.

opposite, clockwise from left: simple sweet and sour mango chutney, tomato chutney and date and tamarind chutney

ingredients
300 ml (½ pint) natural yogurt
1 teaspoon sugar
1 teaspoon salt
½ teaspoon mint sauce
1 cucumber, peeled and grated
1 fresh green chilli, finely diced
**1 tablespoon chopped fresh
  coriander**

to garnish:
**½ teaspoon crushed coriander
  seeds**
**½ teaspoon crushed white
  cumin seeds**

*One of the most well-known raitas, I make this with ready-made bottled
mint sauce. The raita has a better texture if you grate the cucumber
although you can just dice it if you wish.*

cucumber and mint **raita**

1 Beat the natural yogurt and place in a serving bowl. Stir in the sugar, salt,
mint sauce, grated cucumber, green chilli and fresh coriander.
2 To serve, garnish the raita with the coriander and cumin seeds.

*I am pleased to see that mooli (also known as white radish, daikon and
Japanese radish) is now readily available at most supermarkets. In this
recipe, both the mooli and the carrots are grated before they are mixed
with the yogurt, and the raita is dressed with seasoned oil.*

mooli and carrot raita

(Mooli Aur Gajar Ka Raita)

1 Beat the yogurt with the sugar, salt, green chillies, fresh coriander and mint,
then beat in the measured water. Turn into a serving bowl and stir in the mooli
and carrots.
2 To make the dressing, heat the oil in a small saucepan, add the curry leaves,
mixed white cumin and onion seeds and fry for 1 minute. While still hot pour
the dressing on to the yogurt. Serve garnished with a sprig of mint.

ingredients
300 g (10 oz) natural yogurt
1 teaspoon sugar
1 teaspoon salt
**2 fresh green chillies, finely
chopped**
**2 tablespoons chopped fresh
  coriander**
**1 tablespoon chopped fresh
  mint**
125 ml (4 fl oz) water
**1 small mooli, peeled and
  grated**
2 carrots, grated
sprig of mint, to garnish

seasoned oil dressing:
2 tablespoons corn oil
**6 whole fresh or dried curry
  leaves**
**½ teaspoon mixed white cumin
  seeds and onion seeds**

opposite, clockwise from left: spicy vegetable raita, mooli and carrot raita and potato and tomato raita

spicy vegetable **raita**

(Masala Dar Subzee Ka Raita)

1 Beat the yogurt with the water and place in a serving bowl.
2 Heat the corn oil in a pan, add the spring onions, cumin seeds and coriander seeds and fry for about 30 seconds, stirring all the time. Lower the heat, add the crushed red chillies, garam masala, aubergine, tomatoes, courgette and salt and stir-fry for 3–5 minutes or until the vegetables are cooked. Finally, add the mint and fresh coriander. Pour the vegetables over the yogurt and stir in.
3 Garnish with more fresh coriander and mint, if desired.

ingredients
500 ml (17 fl oz) natural yogurt
50 ml (2 fl oz) water
2 tablespoons corn oil
1 bunch spring onions, chopped
1 teaspoon cumin seeds
**½ teaspoons crushed
    coriander seeds**
**½ teaspoons crushed dried
    red chillies**
½ teaspoon garam masala
1 small aubergine, diced
2 tomatoes, diced
1 courgette, thinly sliced
1 teaspoon salt
**1 tablespoon chopped fresh
    mint**
**1 tablespoon chopped fresh
    coriander**
**sprigs of mint and coriander,
    to garnish (optional)**

ingredients
**8–10 baby potatoes, halved
    and boiled**
**18–20 cherry tomatoes, halved
    and grilled**
300 ml (½ pint) natural yogurt
1 fresh green chilli
**2 tablespoons roughly chopped
    fresh coriander**
**1 tablespoon roughly chopped
    fresh mint**
½ teaspoon salt
2 tablespoons olive oil
¼ teaspoon cumin seeds
3 whole garlic cloves, peeled
3 whole dried red chillies
6–8 curry leaves
**¼ teaspoon mixed mustard
    seeds and onion seeds**

Made with baby potatoes and cherry tomatoes, and dressed with seasoned oil, this raita makes a tasty and very attractive side dish for a dinner party.

potato and tomato raita

1 Arrange the baby potatoes and cherry tomatoes on a shallow serving dish.
2 Place the yogurt, green chilli, half of the fresh coriander, the fresh mint and salt in a food processor and blend until smooth. Pour over the potatoes and tomatoes.
3 Heat the olive oil in a frying pan, add the cumin seeds, garlic, red chillies, curry leaves, mustard and onion seeds and fry for 1–2 minutes. Pour the spice mixture over the yogurt. Serve garnished with the remaining fresh coriander.

A kachumer is a simple salad of diced vegetables in a lemon-flavoured dressing which provides a refreshing contrast as an accompaniment to any Indian main dish.

kachumer

1 Place the cucumber, tomatoes, onion, carrot, chilli and fresh coriander in a serving bowl, sprinkle with the salt and lemon juice and toss together. Garnish with mint sprigs and serve immediately.

ingredients
½ cucumber, diced
2 tomatoes, deseeded and diced
1 onion, diced
1 carrot, diced
1 fresh green chilli, sliced
2 tablespoons chopped fresh coriander
½ teaspoon salt
2 tablespoons lemon juice
sprigs of fresh mint, to garnish

This naan from Peshawar in Pakistan is becoming increasingly popular in restaurants. It has a sweet filling and, when eaten with any curry, it adds a delicious sweet and sour flavour. It is definitely one of my favourite naans. This recipe makes 6–8 naans.

peshawari **naan**

1 First, blend together all the ingredients for the filling and set aside.
2 To make the dough, put the sugar and the yeast into a cup with the warm water and stir well until the yeast has dissolved. Set aside for 10 minutes or until the mixture is frothy.
3 Sift the flour into a large mixing bowl. Make a well in the centre, add the ghee and salt and pour in the yeast mixture. Mix well using your hands and adding more water if required. Turn the dough on to a floured surface and knead for 5 minutes or until smooth. Return the dough to the bowl, cover and leave to rise in a warm place for 1½ hours or until doubled in size.
4 Turn the dough on to a lightly floured surface and knead for 2 minutes.
5 Break off small pieces of the dough with your hand and pat into rounds about 12 cm (5 inches) in diameter and 1 cm (½ inch) thick. Spread about 1 teaspoon of the filling on top of each naan. Fold each naan in half and roll gently with a rolling pin.
6 Place each naan on a greased sheet of foil and cook under a preheated very hot grill for 7 10 minutes, turning twice to brush with melted butter. Keep wrapped in foil until required.

ingredients
1 teaspoon sugar
1 teaspoon fresh yeast
150–175 ml (5–6 fl oz) warm water
250 g (8 oz) plain flour, plus extra for dusting
1 tablespoon ghee
1 tablespoon salt
75 g (3 oz) unsalted butter, melted

filling:
125 g (4 oz) desiccated coconut
25 g (1 oz) ground almonds
25 g (1 oz) caster sugar
2 tablespoons milk

Breads are an important part of Indian cookery and paratas are cooked almost daily in Indian households. In Indian cafés these paratas are deep-fried in very large karahis and served with freshly barbecued kebabs.

deep-fried **paratas**

1 Sift the flour into a mixing bowl and add the salt. Make a well in the centre and gradually stir in the measured water to make a soft, pliable dough.
2 Divide the dough into 6–8 portions and roll them out on a floured surface.
3 Brush the centre of each parata with about ¼ teaspoon ghee. Fold the dough in half, flatten with the palm of your hand, then place a further ¼ teaspoon ghee in the centre and fold the dough in half again. Form each parata into a ball, then roll out again to a circle, about 18 cm (7 inches) in diameter, dusting with flour as necessary.
4 Heat a thawa or heavy-based frying pan and heat the ghee. Add the paratas one at a time and cook gently for about 30 seconds. Remove from the heat and serve warm.

ingredients
250 g (8 oz) wholemeal flour, plus extra for dusting
½ teaspoon salt
about 200 ml (7 fl oz) water
125 g (4 oz) pure or vegetable ghee

This is one of the less fattening Indian breads as it does not contain any fat, although some people like to brush it with a little melted butter before serving. Ideally chapatis should be eaten as soon as they come off the thawa or out of the frying pan, but if that is not practical keep them warm by wrapping them in foil. In India chapatis are sometimes cooked on a naked flame, which makes them puff up. Allow about 2 per person.

chapati

1 Sift the flour into a mixing bowl with the salt. Make a well in the centre and gradually stir in the measured water, mixing well with your fingers to form a supple dough. Knead for about 7–10 minutes then cover and set aside for 15–20 minutes.
2 Divide the dough into 10–12 pieces and roll them out on a well-floured surface to 15 cm (6 inches) in diameter. Have some foil ready so that you can wrap up the cooked chapatis to keep them warm.
3 Heat a thawa or heavy-based frying pan over a high heat. When it is very hot, lower the heat to medium, place a chapati in the thawa and when it bubbles turn it over. Press down with a clean tea towel or a flat spoon and turn once again. Remove from the pan and keep warm in the foil. Repeat with the other chapatis.

ingredients
250 g (8 oz) wholemeal flour (ata or chapati flour), plus extra for dusting
½ teaspoon salt
200 ml (7 fl oz) water

opposite, clockwise from top: chapati, peshawari naan and deep-fried paratas

A delicious snack at any time of the day, these bhajias should be served with the spicy Tomato Chutney (see page 106) or the Date and Tamarind Chutney (see page 105). The bhajias are made with a light thin gram flour batter, and pomegranate seed powder is added to the batter to give it a tangy flavour.

fried potato slices in a light gram flour batter

(Aloo Bhajias)

1 Sift the gram flour into a large bowl. Add the cumin seeds, crushed red chillies, salt, bicarbonate of soda, pomegranate seed powder, fresh green and red chillies and fresh coriander and stir to mix. Add sufficient water to form a thin batter which will thinly coat the potatoes.

2 Heat the oil in a deep frying pan. Dip the potato slices one at a time into the batter and then fry in the hot oil. Lift out with a slotted spoon and allow to drain on kitchen paper before serving.

ingredients
125 g (4 oz) gram flour
1 teaspoon white cumin seeds
**1 teaspoon crushed dried
    red chillies**
1 teaspoon salt
**½ teaspoon bicarbonate
    of soda**
**1½ teaspoons pomegranate
    seed powder**
1 fresh green chilli, chopped
1 fresh red chilli, chopped
**1 tablespoon chopped fresh
    coriander**
**300–450 ml (½–¾ pint)
    water**
oil, for deep-frying
**2 potatoes, peeled and cut into
    5 mm (¼ inch) slices**

The large aubergines available in most supermarkets are very watery and not as flavoursome as the smaller ones sold by most Asian grocers. For this dish, I recommend two medium-sized aubergines of the smaller variety.

baigun **ka bhurta**

1 Beat the yogurt and measured water with the salt, sugar, garam masala, chilli powder, fresh coriander, mint and green chillies. Pour into a serving dish and set aside.

2 Place the aubergines in a preheated oven, 180°C (350°F), Gas Mark 4, and bake for 10–15 minutes or until the skins can be peeled off easily. Peel the aubergines and cut them into small pieces.

3 Combine the aubergines with the tomatoes, then turn them into the yogurt mixture. Mix thoroughly before serving.

ingredients
300 ml (½ pint) natural yogurt
125 ml (4 fl oz) water
1 teaspoon salt
½ teaspoon sugar
1 teaspoon garam masala
1 teaspoon chilli powder
**2 tablespoons chopped fresh
    coriander**
1 teaspoon chopped fresh mint
**2 fresh green chillies, finely
    chopped**
**2 aubergines, topped and
    tailed**
**2 tomatoes, deseeded and
    chopped**

dumplings in a sweet and sour yogurt sauce with tamarind sauce

(Dahi Vadas)

ingredients
250 g (8 oz) urid dhaal powder
1 teaspoon baking powder
1 teaspoon ground ginger
1 teaspoon finely chopped fresh coriander
1 small fresh green chilli, finely chopped
450 ml (¾ pint) water
oil, for deep-frying
475 ml (16 fl oz) natural yogurt
1 teaspoon sugar
1 teaspoon salt
sprigs of coriander, to garnish

tamarind sauce:
1 tablespoon tamarind paste
½ teaspoon ground ginger
1 teaspoon sugar
½ teaspoon salt
150 ml (¼ pint) water

1 Place the urid dhaal powder in a mixing bowl with the baking powder, ginger, fresh coriander and green chilli. Add 300 ml (½ pint) of the measured water and mix to make a thick batter.
2 Heat the oil in a karahi or large saucepan, add the batter about 1 teaspoon at a time and deep-fry the dumplings until golden brown.
3 Remove with a slotted spoon and drain on kitchen paper.
4 In a separate bowl, mix the yogurt with the remaining water, sugar and salt and whisk with a fork. Drop the dumplings into the yogurt and stir to coat them all over.
5 To make the tamarind sauce, put the tamarind paste, ginger, sugar, salt and measured water in a bowl and stir to make a thick sauce. Taste the sauce and if it is too sour or thick, add more sugar or water. Pour the sauce over the dahi vadas and serve garnished with fresh coriander.

fried eggs with tomatoes and peppers

ingredients
2 tablespoons corn oil
1 onion, sliced into rings
½ red pepper, cored, deseeded and sliced
½ green pepper, cored, deseeded and sliced
2 tomatoes, sliced
1 tablespoon chopped fresh coriander
4 eggs
¼ teaspoon salt
6 black peppercorns, freshly ground
2 fresh green chillies, chopped

1 Heat the oil in a large frying pan. Spread the onion rings in the pan and fry for about 1½ minutes, then add the sliced peppers, tomatoes and half of the fresh coriander and cook for 3–5 minutes.
2 Break the eggs side by side into the pan and sprinkle with the salt and pepper. Gently shake the pan without breaking the yolks and spoon some of the hot oil over the eggs to cook them.
3 To serve, sprinkle with the remaining fresh coriander and the green chillies. Serve immediately with toasted granary bread.

Serve this spicy scrambled egg dish for a late breakfast with freshly made paratas and a mango chutney.

spicy egg curry

(Khageena)

ingredients
4 tablespoons corn oil
2 curry leaves (optional)
2 onions, finely diced
½ teaspoon garlic pulp
½ teaspoon ginger pulp
1 teaspoon crushed dried red chillies
1 tomato, sliced
2 fresh green chillies, chopped
1 tablespoon chopped fresh coriander
1 teaspoon salt
6 eggs

1 Heat the oil in a large heavy-based frying pan, add the curry leaves, if using, with the onions, garlic, ginger and dried chillies, fry for about 2 minutes.
2 Add the tomato and green chillies and stir-fry for about 30 seconds, then add the fresh coriander, salt and eggs. Break the egg yolks and then stir the eggs into the tomato and spices, stir-fry for a further 2 minutes. Serve immediately.

desserts and drinks

There are a number of Indian sweet desserts which do not seem to have found their way on to restaurant menus. Rice pudding is probably one of the most popular desserts in India and Pakistan.

rice **pudding**

(Chawal Ki Kheer)

1 Wash the Basmati rice thoroughly and place in a large saucepan. Pour in 900 ml (1½ pints) of the milk and bring to the boil. Add the green cardamoms and cook over a very low heat for 15–20 minutes until the milk has been absorbed by the rice.
2 Remove the pan from the heat and, using a wooden masher, mash the rice making swift circular movements in the pan for at least 5 minutes. Return to the heat, gradually stir in the remaining milk and bring to the boil, stirring occasionally. Add the sugar and saffron and cook, stirring, for 7–10 minutes or until the pudding has a good thick consistency.
3 Transfer the rice pudding to a serving dish and decorate with the flaked almonds and varq.

ingredients
75 g (3 oz) Basmati rice
1.5 litres (2½ pints) milk
3 green cardamoms
250 g (8 oz) sugar
¼ teaspoon saffron strands

to decorate:
½ teaspoon flaked almonds
varq (silver leaf, see page 13)

Lassi is a drink which originated in roadside cafés in the Punjab and which, over the years, has become very popular all over India and Pakistan. In the past, it was made with natural yogurt and served garnished with malai (the skin that forms on top of milk when it is boiled). However, these days you will find a number of flavours such as mango, pistachio and sweet and sour. The rose-flavoured version, which is a particular favourite of mine, has a beautiful aroma. Deliciously cool on a hot summer's day, it also aids the digestion of spicy food.

rose-flavoured **lassi**

1 Pour the rose syrup, natural yogurt and sugar into a food processor or blender and whisk for about 1 minute. Add the milk and the water and work for 1 further minute.
2 Pour the lassi into individual glasses and serve topped with ice cubes and fresh rose petals.

ingredients
2 tablespoons sweetened rose syrup
300 ml (½ pint) natural yogurt
2 tablespoons sugar
300 ml (½ pint) milk
600 ml (1 pint) water

to serve:
ice cubes
fresh rose petals

previous page, clockwise from left: rice pudding, rose-flavoured lassi and sweet dumplings

These sweet dumplings, or gulgulay, are made mostly for wedding ceremonies. They are very easy to make, however, and ideally they should be served warm.

sweet **dumplings**
(Gulgulay)

1 Sift the flour, ground almonds and sugar into a large bowl, then add the flaked almonds and sultanas. Stir in the milk and make a thick batter.
2 Heat the ghee or oil in a deep frying pan, drop the batter, 1 teaspoonful at a time, into the hot oil and fry for 35–40 seconds, turning at least once until golden brown. Using a slotted spoon, remove the dumplings and drain on kitchen paper. Serve warm.

ingredients
50 g (2 oz) self-raising flour
4 tablespoons ground almonds
75 g (3 oz) sugar
1 tablespoon flaked almonds
1 tablespoon sultanas
200 ml (7 fl oz) milk
oil or ghee, for deep-frying

This halva is a traditional recipe made for stuffing pears which were then deep-fried and served with kheer (rice pudding). However, it is also delicious on its own, warm with fresh cream.

chana dhaal dessert
(Chanay Ki Dhaal Ka Halva)

ingredients
10 tablespoons chana dhaal
900 ml (1½ pints) water
6 tablespoons pure or
** vegetable ghee**
3 green cardamoms
3 whole cloves
6 tablespoons ground almonds
1 teaspoon saffron strands
50 g (2 oz) sultanas
12 tablespoons caster sugar

to decorate:
flaked almonds
varq (silver leaf, see page 13)

1 Ideally the chana dhaal should be soaked for about 3 hours before boiling. However, if this is not possible, wash the lentils and place them in a large saucepan with the water and boil over a medium heat for 15–20 minutes until all the water has evaporated and the dhaal is soft enough to be mashed into a paste. (You can purée the dhaal in a food processor.)
2 Heat the ghee in a separate large saucepan, then add the cardamoms and cloves. Lower the heat and add the chana dhaal paste and stir and mix together using the bhoonoing method (see page 9) for 5–7 minutes.
3 Gradually fold in the ground almonds, saffron, sultanas and the sugar, stirring continuously. By now the halva should have thickened and darkened in colour. Continue stirring the mixture for a further 7–10 minutes, reducing the heat if necessary.
4 Remove from the heat, transfer to a serving dish and decorate with flaked almonds and varq. Serve hot or cold.

Since the advent of food processors, it has become extremely easy to make desserts like this one, which require a lot of grating – in this case, a large quantity of grated carrot. As the halva freezes very well, it is worth making it in a fairly large quantity. It is a very sweet dessert, quite a contrast after spicy food.

Varq, which is very finely beaten silver leaf, is used to decorate food on special occasions. It is sold interleaved with sheets of plain paper. To use, you simply place the varq on the food and remove the protective paper. If necessary, sprinkle the varq with a few drops of water.

carrot **halva**

ingredients
10 tablespoons vegetable ghee
1.5 kg (3 lb) carrots, grated
250 ml (8 fl oz) evaporated milk
4 green cardamoms
50 g (2 oz) sultanas
8–10 tablespoons sugar
250 g (8 oz) ground almonds
double cream, to serve

to decorate:
25 g (1 oz) flaked almonds
25 g (1 oz) shelled pistachio nuts
2 leaves varq (silver leaf, see page 13)

1 Heat the ghee in a large heavy-based saucepan. Add the grated carrots and stir-fry for about 15 minutes or until the moisture from the carrots has evaporated and the carrots have darkened slightly in colour. Add the evaporated milk, cardamoms, sultanas, sugar and ground almonds and stir-fry for a further 15–20 minutes, using the bhoonoing method (see page 9), until the halva is a rich brownish-red colour.
2 Transfer the halva to a shallow dish and decorate with the flaked almonds, pistachio nuts and varq.
3 Serve warm with a generous helping of double cream.

opposite: carrot halva

I call this a dessert as it is almost always served as part of a brunch, usually at the end. It is delicious with paratas, but if you feel lazy you can serve it with fresh toast.

ground almond dessert

(Badaam Ka Hareera)

1 Heat the vegetable ghee in a haandi or a heavy-based saucepan. Add the flour and stir continuously with a large whisk to prevent any lumps forming.
2 Still stirring, add the ground almonds, about 2 tablespoonfuls at a time. Lower the heat slightly to prevent burning and continue to stir until the almonds colour a little.
3 Remove the pan from the heat and gradually stir in the milk, stirring continuously. Return the pan to a moderate heat and cook for 5–7 minutes, stirring almost constantly with a whisk.
4 Taste the dessert to see how sweet it is and stir in the sugar according to taste, then cook until it has thickened to the consistency of a thick cream soup. Serve hot in small bowls.

ingredients
2 tablespoons vegetable ghee
1 tablespoon ata (chapati flour)
8–10 tablespoons ground almonds
750 ml (1¼ pints) milk
3–4 tablespoons sugar

A traditional Hyderabadi dessert which is served with either vanilla custard or fresh cream. Either way it is delicious and will be very popular with your guests at a dinner party. The correct apricots to use for this recipe are those sold at Asian grocers which are different and more suitable than the ones available at most health shops.

apricot **dessert**

(Qurbani Ka Meetha)

1 Place the apricots in a saucepan with the water and sugar and cook over a low heat for 15–20 minutes until they are soft and the syrup has thickened.
2 Turn the custard into a serving bowl, cover and chill.
3 Pour the softened apricots and their syrup into the chilled custard and serve with the fresh cream.

ingredients
250 g (8 oz) dried apricots, halved and stoned
600 ml (1 pint) water
5 tablespoons sugar
425 g (14 oz) carton ready-made vanilla custard
50 ml (2 fl oz) fresh cream, to serve

This is one of the most popular Indian sweetmeats. 'Gulab' means rose and the flavour and beautiful aroma of this sweetmeat comes from rose-water. The finished dish can be served hot or cold and makes a delicious dinner party dessert served with cream.

deep-fried
sweetmeats in syrup

(Gulab Jamun)

1 Place the milk powder, flour and baking powder in a bowl. Add the melted butter and egg and blend with a fork. Add the milk, if necessary, to form a soft dough. Break the dough into about 12 small pieces and shape into small, smooth balls in the palm of your hands.
2 Heat the ghee in a deep frying pan or karahi, lower the heat and fry the balls about 3–4 at a time, turning them gently with a slotted spoon until a dark golden brown. Remove from the pan and set aside in a deep serving bowl.
3 To make the syrup, boil the water with the sugar in a heavy-based saucepan for 7–10 minutes. Add the crushed cardamom seeds and saffron, then pour over the gulab jamuns. Pour the rose-water on top. Allow about 10 minutes for the gulab jamuns to soak up some of the syrup before serving.

ingredients
- **5 tablespoons dried full cream milk powder**
- **1½ tablespoons plain flour**
- **1 teaspoon baking powder**
- **1½ teaspoons unsalted butter, melted**
- **1 egg, beaten**
- **1 teaspoon milk, to mix (if required)**
- **10 tablespoons pure or vegetable ghee**
- **2 tablespoons rose-water**

syrup:
- **750 ml (1¼ pints) water**
- **8 tablespoons sugar**
- **2 green cardamoms, peeled with seeds crushed**
- **1 large pinch saffron strands**

This is a quick and easy way of turning an ordinary vanilla ice cream into an unusual and delicious mango one. It is served with sliced bananas and whipped cream.

quick mango and
banana split

1 Turn the mango pulp into a bowl, add the sugar and blend well. Place the ice cream in a freezerproof bowl. Pour 300 g (10 oz) of the mango pulp into the ice cream and whisk well with a fork. Cover and place in the freezer until required.
2 To serve, remove the ice cream from the freezer and place 2 scoops on each of 4 dessert plates. Arrange the bananas on the plates and decorate the mango splits with the remaining mango pulp, the pistachio nuts, wafers, curls and whipped cream.

ingredients
- **1 x 425 g (14 oz) can mango pulp**
- **2 tablespoons sugar**
- **500 ml (17 fl oz) vanilla ice cream**
- **4 small bananas, sliced lengthways**

to decorate:
- **2 tablespoons crushed pistachio nuts**
- **4 wafers**
- **8 light crisp curls**
- **125 ml (4 fl oz) whipped cream**

Only use the sweetened rose syrup which is available from most Indian and Pakistani grocers and supermarkets. I am sure you will enjoy this easily made refreshing milk shake.

rose-flavoured milk
with ice cream

ingredients
**3–4 tablespoons sweetened
   rose syrup**
600 ml (1 pint) chilled milk
300 ml (½ pint) chilled water
1 tablespoon sugar
3–4 scoops vanilla ice cream

1 Pour the rose syrup, milk, water and sugar into a food processor or blender and whisk for about 1½ minutes. Pour into individual glasses and add a scoop of ice cream. Serve immediately.

Iced water is always served with Indian meals, but refreshing soft drinks are popular, too. This is an excellent drink for hot summer days. Although I have suggested you use carbonated water, it is equally delicious made with still water.

ingredients
juice of 3–4 limes
6–8 tablespoons caster sugar
**900 ml (1½ pints) carbonated
   water**

to serve:
ice cubes
lime slices
sprigs of mint

lime **sherbert**

1 Pour the lime juice into a large jug. Add the sugar and stir thoroughly until the sugar has dissolved completely. Add the carbonated water and stir to mix for about 2 minutes. Chill until required.
2 To serve, top with ice cubes and lime slices and decorate with mint sprigs.

Choose nice ripe mangoes for this recipe as they have to be mashed. When fresh mangoes are not available, use canned mango pulp mixed with milk. Incidentally, mango pulp makes a delicious sauce for any ice cream. See page 123 for a recipe for Quick Banana and Mango Split.

mango **milkshake**

ingredients
3 ripe mangoes, peeled, stoned and roughly chopped
600 ml (1 pint) milk
2–3 tablespoons sugar, depending on the sweetness of the mangoes
1 tablespoon Greek yogurt

1 Place the chopped mangoes in an electric juicer or food processor and whisk for 1 minute or until they begin to look like pulp. Add the milk and sugar to taste and whisk again for 1 minute. Add the Greek yogurt and whisk for 1 further minute until the mixture becomes frothy. Pour into individual glasses and serve chilled or with ice cubes.

This delicately spiced tea is very warming (my mother always gave it to me when I had a cold) and is a fragrant alternative to coffee after a meal. Serve it with or without sugar.

spicy **tea**

ingredients
300 ml (½ pint) milk
300 ml (½ pint) water
2 teabags
2 cinnamon sticks
2 green cardamoms
1 clove
sugar, to serve (optional)

1 Put the milk and water into a saucepan and bring to the boil, then add the teabags. Lower the heat and add the cinnamon, cardamoms and clove. Bring slowly back to the boil and boil for 3–5 minutes. Strain into a teapot, discarding the spices. Serve with or without sugar.

index